AMERICAN ★ HISTORY

The Story of the CONSTITUTION
Creating the U.S. Government

By Leslie Beckett

Portions of this book originally appeared in *The Constitution and Founding of America* by John M. Dunn.

LUCENT PRESS

Published in 2017 by
Lucent Press, an Imprint of Greenhaven Publishing, LLC
353 3rd Avenue
Suite 255
New York, NY 10010

Designer: Deanna Paternostro
Editor: Katie Kawa

Cataloging-in-Publication Data

Names: Beckett, Leslie.
Title: The Story of the Constitution: creating the U.S. government / Leslie Beckett.
Description: New York : Lucent Press, 2017. | Series: American history | Includes index.
Identifiers: ISBN 9781534560444 (library bound) | ISBN 9781534560437 (ebook)
Subjects: LCSH: United States. Constitution--Juvenile literature. | Constitutional law--United States--Juvenile literature. | Constitutional history--Juvenile literature.
Classification: LCC KF4550.Z9 B43 2017 | DDC 342.7302'9--dc23
Printed in the United States of America

CPSIA compliance information: Batch #CW17KL: For further information contact Greenhaven Publishing LLC, New York, New York at 1-844-317-7404.

Please visit our website, www.greenhavenpublishing.com. For a free color catalog of all our high-quality books, call toll free 1-844-317-7404 or fax 1-844-317-7405.

Contents

Foreword	4
Setting the Scene: A Timeline	6
Introduction: An Experiment in Democracy	8
Chapter One: Creating an American Identity	12
Chapter Two: Opposing Tyranny	26
Chapter Three: Fighting for Liberty	37
Chapter Four: Governing the New Nation	51
Chapter Five: The Constitutional Convention	62
Chapter Six: Debating the Document	77
Epilogue: Challenges and Changes	86
Notes	92
For More Information	96
Index	98
Picture Credits	103
About the Author	104

Foreword

The United States is a relatively young country. It has existed as its own nation for more than 200 years, but compared to nations such as China that have existed since ancient times, it is still in its infancy. However, the United States has grown and accomplished much since its birth in 1776. What started as a loose confederation of former British colonies has grown into a major world power whose influence is felt around the globe.

How did the United States manage to develop into a global superpower in such a short time? The answer lies in a close study of its unique history. The story of America is unlike any other—filled with colorful characters, a variety of exciting settings, and events too incredible to be anything other than true.

Too often, the experience of history is lost among the basic facts: names, dates, places, laws, treaties, and battles. These fill countless textbooks, but they are rarely compelling on their own. Far more interesting are the stories that surround those

basic facts. It is in discovering those stories that students are able to see history as a subject filled with life—and a subject that says as much about the present as it does about the past.

The titles in this series allow readers to immerse themselves in the action at pivotal historical moments. They also encourage readers to discuss complex issues in American history—many of which still affect Americans today. These include racism, states' rights, civil liberties, and many other topics that are in the news today but have their roots in the earliest days of America. As such, readers are encouraged to think critically about history and current events.

Each title is filled with excellent tools for research and analysis. Fully cited quotations from historical figures, letters, speeches, and documents provide students with firsthand accounts of major events. Primary sources also bring authority to the text. Sidebars highlight these quotes and primary sources, as well as interesting figures and events. Annotated bibliographies allow students to locate and evaluate sources for further information on the subject.

A deep understanding of America's past is necessary to understand its present and its future. Sometimes you have to look back to see how to best move forward, and that's certainly true when writing the next chapter in the American story.

Setting the Scene:

1607
First British settlement at Jamestown is established.

1630
Puritans establish the Massachusetts Bay Colony.

1649
British king Charles I is found guilty of treason by the British Parliament and executed.

1607 1609 1630 1649 1689

1609
Shakespeare's sonnets are published for the first time.

1689
English philosopher John Locke publishes *An Essay Concerning Human Understanding*.

A Timeline

1775
The Battles of Lexington and Concord mark the official start of the American Revolution.

1789
The Bill of Rights is ratified, George Washington is elected president, and the French Assembly adopts the Declaration of the Rights of Man.

1775 | 1776 | 1783 | 1789 | 1804

1783
The United States and Great Britain sign a peace treaty to formally end the American Revolution.

1776
The United States Congress approves the Declaration of Independence.

1804
Meriwether Lewis and William Clark set out on their exploration of the Louisiana Territory.

Introduction

AN EXPERIMENT IN DEMOCRACY

The The United States is sometimes called a great experiment in democracy. It was founded on the belief that people should have a say in how they are governed and that individual liberty should be protected from tyranny. These beliefs led Americans to fight for their independence from Great Britain, and they also strongly influenced the creation of the U.S. government once independence was achieved.

At the heart of this great experiment in democracy is the U.S. Constitution. It is the oldest national constitution still in use today, and it has been the backbone of the U.S. government for more than 200 years. This document was created to bring 13 different states together under one functional government, and now it unites more than 300 million people in 50 states under one national identity.

Governing a New Nation

The story of the U.S. Constitution began long before the document was written. It has its roots in the long struggle for Americans to govern themselves, which reached a boiling point in 1775. Tensions between the British and the Americans over taxation, representation, and the power of the monarchy turned violent with the Battles of Lexington and Concord, which started the American Revolution. This war ended with the Americans emerging victorious and independent in 1783, but it was not smooth sailing from there.

Governing the new nation was a process of trial and error. The first attempt to unite the colonies under the Articles of Confederation proved to be dangerously ineffective, so U.S. leaders met in Philadelphia, Pennsylvania, in 1787 to come up with a new plan for bringing the American people together under a more effective federal government. After much debate and compromise, the U.S. Constitution was born. Not only did it serve its initial purpose of allowing the young nation to survive in its early years; it served as the strong foundation upon which America grew into a leading world power and symbol of democracy around the globe.

A Living Document

The U.S. Constitution is often referred to as a living document because it has been able to grow and evolve over time. The Founding Fathers anticipated the need to adapt the document to changes in American culture, values, and politics. They created a system for amending the Constitution to reflect these changes. For example, the Constitution did not originally address the concept of slavery. However, it was amended after the American Civil War in 1865 to outlaw the practice throughout the nation. Other amendments have been passed to grant women voting rights, to lower the voting age, and to give all citizens the right to vote, regardless of their race. As such, the

Visitors to the National Archives in Washington, D.C., can see an original copy of the Constitution alongside the Declaration of Independence and the Bill of Rights.

Constitution has changed as the country has changed, becoming more inclusive and giving more Americans a say in how they are governed.

As new challenges arise in America, it can be difficult to interpret how the Constitution applies to situations the Founding Fathers would never have imagined. How does the concept of freedom of the press apply to bloggers on the Internet? Does the Second Amendment to the Constitution, which refers to the right of citizens to bear arms, include military-grade weapons? It is the job of the Supreme Court to decide how the Constitution should be interpreted in modern times and applied to modern situations. Its judgments help keep the spirit of the Constitution alive in a nation that is vastly different from what it was when the document was first written.

An Ongoing Story

Debates over the meaning of parts of the Constitution and the intent of the men who wrote them have existed since the document was still in the process of being ratified, or formally approved. Certain topics in the document are still considered hot topics today—from

The U.S. Supreme Court is tasked with interpreting the Constitution.

states' rights and presidential power to freedom of religion and the Electoral College. The fact that these constitutional issues are still debated today proves that the words of the Founding Fathers remain as important now as they were more than two centuries ago.

The story of the Constitution is far from over. It evolves with every Supreme Court decision and every classroom debate. The Founding Fathers created a document with staying power, and, in doing so, they created a government that continues to reflect the democratic ideals that have been a part of America since its earliest days.

Chapter One

CREATING AN AMERICAN IDENTITY

The United States is known as a nation made of many different groups of people who live and work together. This has been part of the American identity since Native Americans first settled on the continent and developed different cultures based on the places they lived.

As Europeans began to travel to the New World—the name they gave the Americas—they settled in different areas based on the countries they came from and the things they hoped to do and achieve in this new land. As such, different parts of North America developed unique economies, cultures, and even governments. In time, these parts would all unite together as one nation with one identity, which was described by French American writer J. Hector St. John de Crèvecoeur (also known as Michel-Guillaume-Saint-Jean de Crèvecoeur) in his 1782 collection of essays *Letters from an American Farmer*:

> *Here individuals of all nations are melted into a new race of men, whose labours and posterity will one day cause great changes in the world … The Americans were once scattered all over Europe; here they are incorporated into one of the finest systems of population that have ever appeared, and which will hereafter become distinct by the power of the different climates they inhabit.*[1]

The journey to create a uniquely American identity was not an easy one, though. It was challenging from the very beginning, but those challenges helped Americans see themselves as different from those who lived in the countries they left behind.

Europeans in the New World

Although the Vikings are believed to be the first Europeans to reach the Americas as far back as AD 1000, the rush to colonize the New World did not truly start until after Christopher Columbus arrived in 1492, sailing under the Spanish flag. Spain and its neighbor, Portugal, were two of the most powerful countries in the early years of American colonization. Soon, Sweden, the Netherlands, France, England, and Denmark also dispatched small sailing ships for America. Explorers, soldiers, treasure seekers, adventurers, and priests were among the first to arrive. Next came

Interactions between Native Americans and some European settlers were peaceful and friendly. However, in many cases, they were not. Violence and disease came with the Europeans, wiping out large portions of the Native American population and forcing many groups from their homelands.

settlers who farmed, fished, hunted, trapped, and set up communities and commercial enterprises. They carried firearms, farming tools, iron cooking pots, writing utensils, and other items of interest to the Native Americans who were living in the lands the Europeans wanted to control.

Some Europeans befriended and peacefully coexisted with America's native inhabitants, who Columbus mistakenly called the "Indians." All too often, however, encounters between Europeans and Native Americans resulted in violence. Making matters worse, new diseases introduced by the Europeans killed millions of Native Americans. Equipped with superior weapons, horses, and well-trained armies, the ever-growing immigrant population increasingly pushed Native Americans off their homelands and seized those lands for their own use.

By the 17th century, several European nations had a firmly established presence in North America. Spain controlled the lands that are now Texas, California, other areas of the American West, Central America, and much of South America. The Dutch had settled in many areas, including what is now New York. French fur trappers, merchants, and Catholic priests occupied the middle of the North American continent in settlements ranging from Quebec in the north to New Orleans in the south.

Early English Settlements

England, meanwhile, set up thriving colonies along the Atlantic coast. Its first permanent colony was Jamestown, Virginia, which was established in 1607. At first, Jamestown's investors expected to earn a profit by finding valuable metals and other riches. Soon, however, the colony was headed for disaster. Many settlers died from disease and starvation during the first year. If not for the strong leadership of Captain John Smith, the colony would have collapsed. To succeed, the settlers had to abandon seeking gold and instead build a stable community with a new sense of direction and purpose. The colonists tried other ways to earn a profit besides looking for valuable metals. Eventually, they found a cash crop—tobacco.

The settlers who left England for Jamestown did so because they believed they would live more prosperous lives in Virginia. However, they did not wish to forgo their rights as citizens of England. To assure that their status would not change in the New World, the colony's new charter stated that all British people and their children born there "shall have and enjoy all liberties, franchises, and immunities ... as if they had been abiding and born, within our realm of England."[2]

A very different British settlement began far to the north of Virginia in 1620. The men and women who settled there had originally sailed for Virginia on a ship called the *Mayflower*, but stormy weather forced them north to Plymouth, Massachusetts. Although

The Mayflower Compact, shown here being signed by the adult men on the Mayflower, *is considered the first experiment in self-government in what would become the United States.*

the climate there was colder and the land was not as easy to farm as land in Virginia, the voyagers decided to stay where they had landed. Among the 102 people on the *Mayflower* were 35 people who called themselves Pilgrims. They were members of the Puritan movement that strove to "purify" the Church of England of any Catholic traditions and were seeking religious freedom in the New World.

Before leaving the *Mayflower*, 41 men agreed to sign and abide by a covenant with God that required each of them to work and provide for the common good. This Mayflower Compact, as the agreement became known, is considered the first document of self-government created by Europeans in what is now the United States.

The community at Plymouth was later absorbed into the Massachusetts Bay

Colony, which was founded in 1630 by a much larger group of Puritans who escaped persecution in England. Their leader, lawyer John Winthrop, had proclaimed, "We shall be as a city upon a hill. The eyes of all people are upon us."[3]

The 13 British Colonies

Other British colonies were later established, most of them with strong religious ties. Groups of people who did not agree with the way the Massachusetts Bay Colony was being run founded Connecticut and Rhode Island. Others broke away and settled in New Hampshire in 1638. Despite their religious differences, these New England colonies shared many common Protestant beliefs. Religious freedom for Catholics, meanwhile, was the driving force behind the colony of Maryland, which was founded by Lord Baltimore in 1634. In addition, Pennsylvania was settled by members of the religious group known as the Society of Friends, or the Quakers, in 1682.

England also took control of the Dutch colony of New Netherland, which they renamed New York, and New Jersey, which was an area that contained both Dutch and Swedish settlements, in 1664. Delaware, which was another area with Swedish and Dutch settlers, was ruled by the Pennsylvania legislature until 1701. Then, its citizens created their own representative assembly.

To the south of Virginia lay the colony of Carolina, which was later split into North Carolina and South Carolina. Below South Carolina lay Georgia, a colony begun in 1732 by philanthropist James Oglethorpe to serve as a haven for those who would otherwise be imprisoned in England for unpaid debts. Georgia was also a military outpost established to keep watch on its southern neighbor, Florida, which was a Spanish territory at that time.

Altogether, England ruled 13 colonies in what is now the United States, and immigrants poured into them. They were not all from the area we now call the British Isles—England, Wales, Scotland, and Ireland. Immigrants also came from France, Germany, Switzerland, the Netherlands, Sweden, and Finland. The people who settled in the 13 British colonies were eager to leave Europe. They wanted to escape the religious persecution, poverty, and wars that were common at the time. They saw coming to America as a chance to have a fresh start in a place that was far from the problems of the Old World.

Not all immigrants came to America as free people, however. Some sold themselves as indentured servants who were obliged to work for people in the colonies for seven years or longer to pay for their passage. Others were brought to North America against their will. Millions of Africans were captured in their homeland and sold as slaves in the 13 colonies.

Most immigrants lived in towns and villages. However, cities were growing, too. Boston, Newport, New York, Charleston, Salem, Providence,

Philadelphia: A City of "Wonder"

Colonial America's finest city was Philadelphia, as traveler Andrew Burnaby noted in his book *Travels Through the Middle Settlements in North America, in the Years 1759 and 1760*:

> *[Philadelphia] must certainly be the object of every one's wonder and admiration. It is situated upon a tongue of land, a few miles above the confluence of the Delaware and Schuilkill; and contains about 3,000 houses, and 18 or 20,000 inhabitants. It is built north and south upon the banks of the Delaware; and is nearly two miles in length, and three quarters of one in breadth. The streets are laid out with great regularity in parallel lines, intersected by others at right angles, and are handsomely built: on each side there is a pavement of broad stones for [pedestrians]; and in most of them a causeway in the middle for carriages. Upon dark nights it is well lighted, and watched by a patrole: there are many fair houses and public edifices in it.*[1]

1. Quoted in Rebecca Brooks Gruver, *An American History*, 4th ed. New York, NY: Knopf, 1985, p. 64.

Philadelphia was one of the most famous and admired cities in the 13 colonies in the 1700s.

A "Similarity of Speech"

Like many other aspects of the American identity, the American language also evolved into something new during the colonial period. In a letter from America dated June 8, 1770, William Eddis observed a distinctive sameness of speech that was developing and unifying Americans in the process:

> *In England, almost every county is distinguished by a peculiar dialect; even different habits, and different modes of thinking ... but in Maryland, and throughout adjacent provinces, it is worthy of observation, that a striking similarity of speech universally prevails; and it is strictly true, that the pronunciation of the generality of the people has an accuracy and elegance, that cannot fail of gratifying the most judicious ear.*
>
> *The colonists are composed of adventurers, not only from every district of Great Britain and Ireland, but from almost every other European government ... Is it not, therefore, reasonable to suppose, that the English language must be greatly corrupted by such a strange intermixture of various nations? The reverse is, however, true. The language of the immediate descendants of such a promiscuous [mixed] ancestry is perfectly uniform, and unadulterated [uncorrupted]; nor has it borrowed any provincial, or national accent, from its British or foreign parentage.*[1]

1. Quoted in Daniel J. Boorstin, *The Americans: The Colonial Experience*. New York, NY: Random House, 1958, pp. 274–275.

Baltimore, Richmond, and Savannah were becoming important centers of trade and commerce. By 1774, Philadelphia—with 40,000 inhabitants—was the nation's largest and wealthiest city and the second largest city in the British Empire. Philadelphia was a leading intellectual center in the colonies and an important port city.

Regional Differences

By the middle of the 18th century, the 13 colonies had developed into three distinct regions. The northern colonies were also known as the New England colonies. Inhabitants lived in towns and on small farms. Others worked as lumbermen in vast forests or as shipbuilders, whalers, fishermen, and traders in bustling seacoast towns such as Portsmouth, Boston, and Providence.

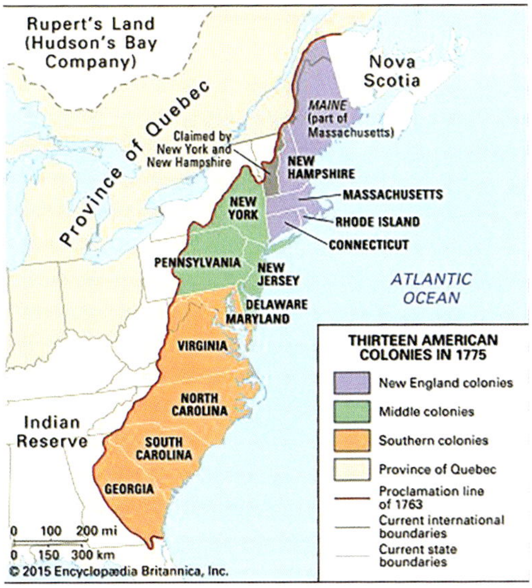

This map shows the regional divisions of the 13 British colonies as they existed in 1775, as well as the western border created by a British proclamation in 1763.

In the middle colonies, meanwhile, fertile land and a moderate climate allowed family farms to produce such large amounts of grain that they became known as the "bread colonies" or "bread basket colonies." Lengthy and navigable rivers, such as the Hudson River and the Delaware River, along with natural harbors in New York City and Philadelphia, promoted trade with other colonies and England.

The economy of the southern colonies, meanwhile, depended on big plantations supported by a large population of black slaves who tended crops of rice, indigo, and tobacco. Much of southern society also mirrored the rigid British social class system. At the top were rich plantation owners whose families lived in mansions. Most southerners, however, were poor white farmers from the British Isles, who dwelled in shacks and cabins on the backwoods frontier. Others worked as carpenters, blacksmiths, bricklayers, bakers, or as artisans, such as architects, woodcarvers, silversmiths, potters, and glassmakers. Black slaves lived at the bottom of the social order.

Shared Experiences and Shared Government

Despite their notable differences, the 13 British colonies had much in common. Colonial homes were commonly clustered together. Sanitation was often poor. Pigs and cattle sometimes roamed the streets. The wilderness was not far away, so colonists who lived in towns could often leave home and soon enter a forest to fish or hunt to supplement their meals. Those who lived far away from the established settlements worried constantly about Native American attacks. In many areas, colonists formed armed militias to provide protection. These experiences prepared many colonists for military action when the American Revolution began.

Most of the colonies were also united by a shared government structure. The king, or someone he selected, picked a governor to run each colony. In turn, the governor chose a council of lawmakers, sometimes called the upper house, to make some of the laws for the colony. A select group of male

King John is shown here signing the Magna Carta, one of the most important documents in British history.

colonists, however, was also allowed to elect the members of the lower house of lawmakers, which was often known as the assembly. At first, most voters and those who held office were either aristocrats or rich landowners. This practice was in accordance with a widely shared conviction that the wealth generated by land ownership enabled an individual to be truly free and not dependent on others for work and money. Such individuals, according to prevailing attitudes, were most fit to govern others.

The Rights of British Citizens

Although colonists lived far from England, most considered themselves British citizens who were entitled to the same rights as citizens who lived across the Atlantic Ocean. These rights dated as far back as 1215 when King John signed the Great Charter, or Magna Carta, a document that required monarchs to obey the rule of law. It also established that accused persons were entitled to a trial by jury and that only Parliament, an elected body, could levy taxes.

In time, British courts and lawmakers guaranteed other rights. By the 17th century, for instance, no citizen could be unreasonably deprived of life, liberty, or property. The Habeas Corpus Act of 1679 stated that arrested persons had a right to receive an official statement of the charges against them and a right to a speedy trial. Another legal provision stipulated that authorities could not search a person's home without a search warrant obtained from a court. The 1689 Bill of Rights asserted that monarchs could exercise certain powers only with the permission of Parliament. Citizens were also entitled to ask their government to solve problems, and they had the right to protection against excessive fines, bails, and cruel and unusual punishments.

Many of the principles reflected in the Magna Carta, the British Bill of Rights, and other foundational documents of British government can also be seen in the U.S. Constitution and other foundational documents of American democracy. Britain

How Were Other Groups Treated?

Though most colonists believed they were entitled to their rights as English citizens, few wanted to extend rights to slaves, Native Americans, or mulattos, which was the name colonists sometimes called people with mixed black and white ancestry. This is made clear in this passage from a 1705 Virginia state statute:

> *And if any slave resist his master, or owner, or other person, by his or her order, correcting such slave, and shall happen to be killed in such correction, it shall not be accounted felony [a serious crime]; but the master, owner, and every such other person so giving correction, shall be free and acquit of all punishment and accusation for the same, as if such accident had never happened: And also, if any negro, mulatto, or Indian, bond or free, shall at any time, lift his or her hand, in opposition against any Christian, not being negro, mulatto, or Indian, he or she so offending, shall, for every such offence, proved by the oath of the party, receive on his or her bare back, thirty lashes, well laid on, cognizable by a justice of the peace for that county wherein such offence shall be committed.*[1]

This passage clearly shows that lawmakers in colonial America did not consider slaves, mulattos, and Native Americans to be deserving of the same legal protection as the white, Christian men who ran the colonies. These men wanted to be treated the same as their fellow British citizens, but they did not want to extend the same sense of equality to people who did not look like them.

1. Quoted in John M. Blum, William S. McFeely, Edmund S. Morgan, Arthur M. Schlesinger Jr., Kenneth M. Stampp, and C. Vann Woodward, *The National Experience: A History of the United States,* 6th ed. San Diego, CA: Harcourt Brace Jovanovich, 1985, p. 63.

influenced the U.S. government even after the United States had become an independent nation.

Law and Punishment

Like other citizens within the British Empire, the colonists also wanted their lives regulated and protected by British common law—a code of legal decisions made by local county courts in England over the centuries. However, because trained lawyers were scarce in the New World, settlers simplified many old legal procedures, and differences between legal rulings and punishments in the colonies and across the Atlantic became more and more common.

For example, capital punishment, or

the death penalty, was handled differently in the British motherland than it was in many of the colonies, with the colonies using it as punishment for far fewer crimes. The use of the death penalty also varied from colony to colony. However, some crimes, such as treason and murder, were punishable by death in nearly all 13 colonies.

A Distinctive Character

Though most Americans considered themselves British citizens, their lives were quite different from those of people in England. Unlike their British counterparts, Americans lived among growing numbers of immigrants, many of whom spoke other languages. These immigrants included Germans, French, Dutch, Scots, Scotch-Irish, and Celtic Irish.

American colonial life was filled with optimism, energy, and drive. Much of this dynamic way of living came from immigrants who, because they were restless and discontent with their old lives in Europe, came to America looking for adventure, opportunity, prosperity, and a new start. Here, they learned to be resourceful on an unknown continent. In time, the colonists developed their own accents, customs, values, and beliefs.

By the mid-18th century, in fact, a distinctive American character had emerged in the colonies. Historian Richard B. Morris noted, "The colonial subjects of George III in 1775 were entirely different from those who had planted Virginia and Plymouth 150 years earlier in James I's reign."[4] These colonial subjects had their own identity as Americans, which was shaped by many factors, including the great physical distance between them and the British subjects who lived in Europe.

Religion in the Colonies

Religion helped forge this new American identity. It provided many Americans with a moral code and a sense

George Whitefield, shown here, was a leader in the religious movement often called the Great Awakening, or First Great Awakening. This religious movement featured outdoor revivals that allowed people from isolated parts of the colonies to join together for a common purpose.

of belonging. However, religion was sometimes the basis for discrimination in colonial America. Though colonists enjoyed more religious tolerance than anywhere in Western Europe, discrimination and persecution were common. For instance, Catholics, Unitarians, and Jews were banned from voting or holding office in several colonies. In addition, many colonists saw no need to separate religion and government. Thus, the Anglican Church, or Church of England, became the official religion of New York, Virginia, Maryland, North Carolina, and South Carolina. The Congregational Church, meanwhile, was the official church of Massachusetts, New Hampshire, and Connecticut. However, no single religion ever reigned as the official religion of all the colonies. In fact, many American congregations exercised local control over their churches rather than yielding to powerful religious authorities, as was the case in England. Some scholars believe such resistance to authority fostered democratic values that later contributed to the American independence movement.

Though many colonists, such as Anglicans and Puritans, were religiously conservative, other Americans, especially those living in rural areas, welcomed the more robust, emotional form of worship encouraged by evangelist preachers. One of the best known was British-born George Whitefield, who traveled across the colonies, holding wild religious jubilees. Enthralled by Whitefield's raucous sermons, congregations laughed, sang, and screamed with joy. Some collapsed and lay shaking on the floor, believing they were in the presence of God's spirit. Known as the Great Awakening, this period of emotionally charged worship spread across the colonies and unintentionally helped prepare isolated American communities for rebellion. It did this by bringing people from remote rural areas together and uniting colonists in a shared experience. British author Paul Johnson wrote, "The Great Awakening's impact … taught different colonies, tidewaters and piedmonts, coast and up country, to grasp and appreciate what they had in common, which was a very great deal."[5] It was also America's first mass movement, which may have helped set the stage for the coming rebellion against political authorities in England.

Colonial Education

Religion also made an impact on American education. Teachers at many schools in the colonies taught Protestant religious beliefs along with the classics and basic academic skills. In 1647, the Massachusetts General Court produced "Old Deluder Laws," which required communities to provide education for children to protect their minds from the powers of Satan—also known as the "Old Deluder."

In addition, many early colonial universities started as religious institutions. Puritans founded Harvard University in 1636 to make sure their congregations would have educated preachers. Yale University was started for the same reason in Connecticut in 1701. In 1746, Presbyterians created what is now known as Princeton University, and Baptists founded what is now Brown University in 1764. Rutgers University was the work of the Dutch Reformed Church. In New York, the Church of England was the benefactor of King's College, now known as Columbia University.

Because Americans lived in a new environment, they developed their own style of education. This gave way to skepticism of those who professed expert academic knowledge, particularly if it was based on ancient, scholarly teachings. American thought "was a way of thinking pervaded by doubt that the professional thinker could think better than others,"[6] according to historian Daniel Boorstin. As such, reading and self-education were widely practiced in the colonies. According to author David McCullough, the 18th century in colonial America was "a day and age that saw no reason why one could not learn whatever was required—learn virtually anything—by the close study of books."[7]

The Enlightenment in America

The American mind was also shaped by the Enlightenment—an ongoing philosophical movement that championed the use of reason and respect for human dignity as a guide to creating a more humane and better-functioning society. The Enlightenment also stressed the need for governments to respect and defend individual rights and the importance of putting restraints on political power. Leaders of this movement believed in a social contract between rulers and those they governed.

Enlightenment writers attacked superstition and unquestioning belief in religious traditions. They also expressed skepticism over a criminal justice system that relied on torture, monarchs who claimed they ruled by divine right, and the powerful influence of organized religion on government. One of the most influential Enlightenment writers, British philosopher John Locke, asserted that all human beings were by their birthright entitled to "natural rights" that no other person could deny. Locke and others advanced the notion that a government had the authority to rule only if those being governed gave their consent. Americans were also impressed with the ideas of Charles-Louis de Secondat, baron de La Brède et de Montesquieu, who is often known only as Montesquieu. He was an Enlightenment writer and thinker who believed that separation of powers helped prevent abuse of government power and protect civil liberties.

Eventually, many of these ideas came into play as Americans revolted against England and formed a new nation. Enlightenment philosophies are reflected in both the Declaration of Independence and the U.S. Constitution.

British leaders, however, did not

Benjamin Franklin, shown here, believed in many Enlightenment ideas and helped them spread throughout the colonies, igniting a spirit of independence in the American people.

embrace the spirit of the Enlightenment the way many colonists did. American inventor, author, scientist, and statesman Benjamin Franklin learned British authority was unyielding when he traveled to London in the 1750s. As a member of the Pennsylvania Assembly, he was told by Earl Granville, lord president of the council, that, "The King in Council is legislator for the Colonies, and when His Majesty's instructions come there, they are the law of the land."[8] Franklin responded that he was unaware that this kind of absolute rule applied to the colonies:

> *I told him this was new doctrine to me. I had always understood from our charters that our laws were to be made by our assemblies to be presented indeed to the King for his royal assent, but that being once given the King could not repeal or alter them. And as our assemblies could not make permanent laws without his assent, [so] neither could he make a law for them without theirs.*[9]

Granville assured Franklin that he was very mistaken, and the incident proved just how wide the gap had become between how Americans wanted to be governed and how British leaders wanted to govern them. This disagreement only added to the growing rift between the British and the colonists, who were continuing to create a strong, independent identity.

Chapter Two

OPPOSING TYRANNY

As the colonists became more united and began developing their own American identity, they started to grow more resentful of being under the rule of another nation, especially one they saw as abusing its power over them. Many Americans started to see British King George III as a tyrant, or an oppressive leader. The opposition to and fear of tyranny that developed in the colonies in the years before the American Revolution helped determine the kind of government Americans created for themselves after the war was over.

How did the colonists change from seeing themselves as British citizens to wanting to stand on their own and rule themselves? The first sparks of rebellion were ignited after a draining war between Britain and France, which created a rift between the colonists and the British that ultimately could not be repaired.

The French and Indian War

The fighting between England and France was part of a series of wars between the two countries for control of Europe and colonial supremacy around the world that began in 1689. In 1754, the fighting spread to North America, where it was called the French and Indian War. At stake was control of the Ohio River Valley, a region both nations wanted to claim for themselves.

When the war began, the colonies sent representatives to meet with 150 Haudenosaunee (also known as Iroquois) leaders in Albany, New York, to work out a mutual defense agreement against the French. It was the first time that the colonies had attempted to create a unified front of any kind. Instead of coming together, however, the delegates bickered and failed to agree on a plan. Their failure disappointed many colonial leaders who realized

The British victory in the French and Indian War was costly in more ways than one.

the importance of the colonies banding together. One of them was Benjamin Franklin, who believed an effective "Albany Plan of Union" could have prevented the war that was to come. He clung to this belief even when he was an old man, saying, "The colonies so united would have been sufficiently strong to have defended themselves. There would then have been no need of troops from England; of course the … [follow-up reasons] for taxing America, and the bloody contest it occasioned, would have been avoided."[10]

The lack of a colonial confederacy, however, did not stop British and colonial troops from overcoming their enemy and winning the French and Indian War. According to the provisions of the 1763 treaty that ended the war, France handed Canada over to Britain, along with all French territory east of the Mississippi River. Because France wanted to reward Spain for its help during the war, it had given Spain the city of New Orleans plus all French lands west of the Mississippi River. Spain had to cede Florida to the British.

Since France was no longer a dominant force in the Americas, England was free to push forward with its territorial ambitions. Little stood in the way of the most powerful empire in the world that now enjoyed a commercial and military presence from the Far East to the New World.

Postwar Problems

British excitement, however, was lessened by a host of new problems. It soon became apparent that the war had divided, rather than united, Americans and the British. Resentment ran high among many colonists who did not want to fight in or pay for a British war. This caused the British to then resent the colonists, whom they saw as being unwilling to pay for their own protection. Historian Francis D. Cogliano explained, "In 1763, the average Briton paid 26 shillings [yearly] in taxes whilst a Massachusetts taxpayer contributed one shilling each year to imperial coffers. Americans, British officials concluded, benefited from the protection afforded by the British army and Royal Navy, and it would only be fair if they contributed to their own defence."[11] The colonists, however, found British demands for money oppressive.

In addition, many colonists were frustrated by the British wartime practice of quartering that required the colonists to feed and shelter British troops in barracks (a later quartering act required the use of colonists' homes). Anger also united many colonists who felt that British officers and England's upper classes treated Americans as inferiors.

British officials had their own complaints. Outraged that Boston merchants had traded with the Spanish and French in the West Indies during the war, Parliament armed British customs officers with writs of assistance—a type of search warrant—that allowed them to inspect Boston warehouses and ships for smuggled, or illegally traded, goods.

Authorities in London were also annoyed by relentless American westward expansion into Native American lands. This was a clear violation of the Royal Proclamation of 1763, which stated that lands west of the Appalachian Mountains were off limits to further settlement by the colonists. British leaders wanted this territory reserved for Native Americans to decrease fighting, but the colonists saw the proclamation as a way to limit their growth. Americans and the British disagreed over how to pay for a military defense against uprisings that resulted when settlers trespassed on Native American lands. British officials gave the colonists a choice: Raise patrols for their own protection, or pay through taxation for British soldiers to get the job done.

Tensions Rise Over Taxes

When the colonies refused to cooperate, Parliament imposed the Sugar Act of 1764 to raise funds. This measure required that colonists pay a tax on imported sugar as well as other goods, such as coffee, wine, and certain kinds of woven cloth. The act also called for the enforcement of the tax on molasses,

The Stamp Act Congress

After the British Parliament passed the Stamp Act, a group of angry American colonial leaders met in New York in 1765. This group is referred to as the Stamp Act Congress, and delegates from nine colonies were present. At this meeting, they created a document referred to as a "Declaration of Rights and Grievances" to express their objections to the Stamp Act. The declaration stated that the colonists should not be taxed without their consent. To do otherwise ignored their rights and basic liberty. This unified response to British authority was something new for the colonists, and it was a sign of what was to come.

which the Sugar Act actually reduced in the hopes that colonists would be more willing to pay it.

One year later, Parliament passed the Stamp Act, a measure that imposed a tax by requiring a stamp to be purchased and placed on all documents, licenses, publications, and even dice in the 13 colonies. Making matters worse, under the Currency Act of 1764, the British insisted that the tax be paid in official British currency and not the paper notes that the colonies had been issuing. The push for this came from British businessmen who feared that American paper money had decreased in value because the colonies had issued too much of it. This refusal to accept paper money, however, placed a great burden on Americans, who had little gold and silver.

Americans were infuriated that they were expected to pay British taxes with a decreasing money supply. Many British officials, meanwhile, were puzzled by the resentment in the colonies. After all, as historian Thomas Fleming noted, "Those Americans, it turns out, had the highest per capita income in the civilized world of their time. They also paid the lowest taxes."[12] However, another force also fueled colonial anger: the widespread conviction that the British government denied the colonies the right to elect their own representatives in Parliament, especially because Parliament was the group that determined their taxes.

British officials scoffed at the suggestion that Americans felt deprived. They pointed out that a very small percentage of all citizens in the British Isles were allowed to vote. Besides, they added, Americans were represented in London because British lawmakers spoke for everyone in the British Empire. The Americans, though, did not agree. They wanted stronger representation if they were expected to pay taxes.

Opposing the Stamp Act

The explanations of the British leaders did nothing to quell the gathering storm in the colonies. When summer came in 1765, the city of Boston erupted with violence. Among the instigators was a secretive and radical group of protesters called the Sons of Liberty, led by brewery owner Samuel Adams. Whenever they could, the Sons of Liberty destroyed the hated stamps and tarred and feathered agents who attempted to collect the tax.

The violence may have had its roots in more than just anger over taxes. Historian Howard Zinn has suggested that an increasing resentment among the poor and working classes in the colonies toward the rich and powerful also played a role in the uprising. Zinn wrote, "In Boston, the economic grievances of the lowest classes mingled with anger against the British and exploded in violence. The leaders of the Independence movement wanted to use that mob energy against England, but also to contain it so that it would not demand too much from them."[13]

This political cartoon shows a funeral for the Stamp Act, which was repealed in 1766.

Angry mobs also attacked the houses of local tax collectors and colonial officials. One witness to the violence was General Thomas Gage, commander of the British forces in North America: "The Boston Mob … attacked, robbed, and destroyed several Houses, and amongst others, that of the Lieutenant Governor."[14] The lieutenant governor Gage spoke of was Thomas Hutchinson, who escaped the mob before they destroyed his home.

Violence was not the only reaction to the new tax. The Stamp Act Congress denounced the taxes and agreed to boycott all British goods. This economic attack on the British proved to be even more successful than the riots in the streets of Boston. Parliament ultimately repealed the Stamp Act in 1766. However, it also passed the Declaratory Act that made clear to Americans that England alone had the right to govern the colonies.

Charles Townshend, shown here, tried to prove Britain's power over the colonies through harsh new laws. However, he only managed to make the colonists angrier and more likely to rebel.

The Townshend Acts

More troubles soon hit the colonies. Charles Townshend, the British chancellor of the exchequer, believed Parliament had been too lenient with the Americans and had not done enough to quell the growing rebellious spirit in the colonies. He led the legislative effort to suspend the New York Assembly for violating the Quartering Act of 1765, which required Americans to provide living quarters for British troops. In addition, Parliament imposed new taxes in 1767 on the colonial importation of lead, paper, and tea to fund British troops in the colonies.

Previously, the colonies lacked a strong feeling of unity. "There was no American nationalism or separatist feeling [from British control],"[15] historian Samuel Eliot Morison has written. In fact, on several occasions, the British government had "intervened to protect minority groups against majorities—Quakers and Anglicans in New England against the dominant Puritans, Delaware against Maryland—Georgia against South Carolina."[16] Now, however, fierce opposition to the so-called "Townshend Acts" united the colonies together as never before. Angry protestors wrote editorials and pamphlets denouncing the British actions. Suspicion ran high that authorities in London intended to suppress the colonies. Colonists formed various patriot groups called committees of correspondence to provide a network of communications to report any British violations of their rights. In addition, colonial leaders once again called for economic boycotts of British goods.

Violence in the Colonies

As anger grew in the colonies, British troops arrived in Boston to keep the peace. For the next year, redcoats—as British troops were called—and local patriots glared at one another on the streets. Finally, tensions boiled over on March 5, 1770, when a small group of Bostonians heaved snowballs at British soldiers and provoked a volley of gunfire that resulted in the death of five Americans. Although the British commander and six of his men later were acquitted of murder charges, local radicals exaggerated the tragedy of the so-called "Boston Massacre" to encourage further unrest in

Patriot leaders used the colonists' anger over the Boston Massacre, shown here, to further their revolutionary cause.

The Boston Massacre

On March 5, 1770, a hostile crowd of Bostonians confronted a unit of British soldiers. The harassed soldiers opened fire on the Bostonians, killing five. Captain Thomas Preston, who was the British officer in charge, provided the following eyewitness account of the event:

> *About 9 [o'clock] some of the guard came to and informed me the town inhabitants were assembling to attack the troops … [A]fter I reached the guard, about 100 people passed in and went toward the custom house where the king's money is lodged. They immediately surrounded the sentry posted there, and with clubs and other weapons threatened to execute their vengeance on him. I was soon informed by a townsman their intention was to carry off the soldier from his post and probably murder him … The mob still increased and [was] more outrageous, striking their clubs or bludgeons one against another, and calling out come on you rascals, you bloody backs, you lobster scoundrels, fire if you dare, … [O]ne of the soldiers having received a severe blow with a stick, stepped a little on one side and instantly fired, on which turning to ask him why he fired without orders, I was struck with a club on my arm, which for some time deprived me of the use of it … [A] general attack was made on the men by a great number of heavy clubs and snow-balls being thrown at them, by which all our lives were in imminent dangers.*[1]

1. Quoted in Steven C. Bullock, *The American Revolution: A History in Documents*. New York, NY: Oxford University Press, 2003, pp. 31–34.

the colonies.

By this point, many London officials realized that Parliament had made a mistake in passing the Townshend Acts. For one thing, British trade had dropped off as a result of British colonial policies. Hostility, rather than obedience, was also widespread across the colonies. Though there was strong support for reversing the latest acts, Parliament did not want to appear cowed by the colonies. To save face, Lord North, the new British chancellor of the exchequer, persuaded Parliament to repeal all recent measures taken against America except the tax on tea.

North's actions brought a period of calm. It was shattered, however, on June 9, 1772, when the British vessel *Gaspee* ran aground searching for smugglers in Narragansett Bay, off the coast of Rhode Island. That night, a group of men from Providence, Rhode Island, boarded the ship, burned it, and shot the captain. A commission dispatched by the British government investigated the matter but uncovered no suspects when local people refused to cooperate.

The Intolerable Acts

Relations between the colonies and England worsened a year later when the East India Company—a British trading company operating in India—tried to avoid economic ruin. Parliament sought to help the company by allowing it to bypass colonial merchants and sell tea directly to Americans. Though the price of tea dropped for consumers, American businessmen lost money. Meanwhile, the British also insisted on collecting a tax on tea—one that they had ignored for many years.

Another revolt soon materialized. On December 16, 1773, a mob of men from Boston—some dressed as Native Americans—boarded ships in Boston Harbor and dumped crates of British tea into the sea. Other protests broke out in

The Boston Tea Party was one of the final steps on the path toward war between Britain and its American colonies.

The First Continental Congress

The initial meeting of the First Continental Congress took place on September 5, 1774. Every colony was represented except Georgia. Their meetings took place in Carpenter's Hall in Philadelphia, and many of the men we consider Founding Fathers, including George Washington and John Adams, were a part of the congress.

During the meetings, the congress drafted the Declaration and Resolves of the First Continental Congress. This document listed the grievances, or complaints, the colonists had concerning Britain's harsh treatment. It also included a bill of rights. The group parted ways in October 1774 but agreed to meet again the following May.

Charleston, New York, and Philadelphia.

News of what we now call the Boston Tea Party outraged Parliament. It retaliated by closing the port of Boston and threatening to keep it sealed under military rule until the colonists paid for the ruined tea, which today would be worth about $1 million. As extra punishment, the British government reduced the powers of the colonial representative assemblies and increased the powers of colonial governors. Parliament also decreed that any royal officers accused of murder would stand trial in London, not America.

To further punish the colonists, British officials extended the southern border of Quebec, Canada—an area typified by French culture but dominated by British rule—to the Ohio River. Not only did this limit American expansion, it also made many Americans fear encroaching French attitudes regarding religion and government. Parliament also imposed a new Quartering Act that required Americans to provide shelter for British troops within their own homes and hotels instead of barracks.

Bostonians were not the only Americans outraged by these actions. Infuriated leaders from most of the other colonies sent delegates to a hastily called meeting of what became known as the First Continental Congress in Philadelphia in September 1774. Here, fiery speakers denounced England's "Intolerable Acts" and urged Americans to boycott all British imports and exports. Radicals, however, failed to convince the Continental Congress to break all ties with England. Most delegates were not ready for such a drastic move. However, the threat of increased violence and organized warfare grew stronger, and leaders on both sides of the Atlantic Ocean prepared for battle.

Lexington and Concord

Though many in Parliament now expected war, they mistakenly believed that their enemy was limited to rebels in Massachusetts. General Thomas Gage, who was now the military governor of Massachusetts, knew better and sent warnings to London that all the colonies were prepared to fight. He also insisted that he needed 20,000 troops to put down the rising rebellion. King George III, however, dismissed Gage's concerns.

By April 1775, informers had alerted Gage that colonial patriots were stockpiling guns and ammunition at Concord, a town outside Boston. After careful planning, British redcoats marched to seize the hidden weapons. Before dawn, patriot horseback riders, including the famous Paul Revere, galloped across the countryside, alerting the local militia that British troops were on the move.

Armed militiamen confronted British troops as they rode through the town of Lexington, Massachusetts. Shots rang out, sparking a gun battle. Moments later, eight Americans lay dead, and Gage's men hurried on to Concord. Along the way, militiamen harassed them with hit-and-run tactics.

By the time the fighting ended at Lexington and Concord, the British had suffered more than 270 casualties; the Americans suffered fewer than 100. The American Revolution had begun.

Chapter Three

FIGHTING FOR LIBERTY

The British had hoped to keep the rebellion confined to Massachusetts, but they could not prevent it from spreading to the rest of the colonies. As the news of the fighting in Lexington and Concord spread, so did the spirit of revolution. People who had grown tired of the oppressive British rule took up arms and joined the rebel—or patriot—cause. However, many colonists still remained loyal to Britain and did not want to wage war. They found themselves torn between their ties to their motherland and their identity as Americans.

On May 10, 1775, colonial leaders gathered again in Philadelphia for the first meeting of what is now called the Second Continental Congress. As the fighting continued in Massachusetts and was beginning to spread to other colonies, it became clear that these leaders were going to have to come up with a plan not just to conduct a war against a world power, but also to unify 13 separate colonies in order to emerge victorious. Shaken by the ongoing violence, the delegates created America's first independent centralized government. Independence was not their initial aim, but it soon became their only option.

Leading the Troops

On the same day as the Second Continental Congress's first meeting, American forces led by Ethan Allen, Benedict Arnold, and a militia group called the Green Mountain Boys occupied Fort Ticonderoga, New York, and seized British cannons. Under the supervision of Henry Knox, American troops transported the weapons across mountains and rivers to help General George Washington, whose forces waited outside of Boston. Washington was respected by his peers, including the members

George Washington did not come from Massachusetts, which was where the American Revolution began. Instead, he was a Virginian. Members of the Second Continental Congress believed his leadership would help unite the colonies and inspire men from Virginia and other areas to join the American cause.

of the Second Continental Congress. One of the new government's first official acts was to take charge of the militia forces fighting in Massachusetts and put them under his command.

As the new leader of the Continental, or American, army, Washington's job was to turn the volunteers into disciplined fighters. Though a widely trusted military leader, Washington insisted that he was not qualified for the position, as he made clear in an acceptance speech addressed to John Hancock during a session of the Continental Congress:

> *I am truly sensible of the high honor done me in this appointment, yet I feel great distress from a consciousness that my abilities and military experience may not be equal to the extensive and important trust. However, as the Congress desire it, I will enter upon the momentous duty and exert every power I possess in the service and for the support of the glorious Cause … [yet] … I do not think myself equal to the command I [am] honored with.*[17]

Despite Washington's concerns, he became a leading figure during the American Revolution and the early years of the new nation it created. The delegates voted to support Washington's troops with paper money and then turned to other urgent issues. At this point, radicals demanded an immediate break with England, but many other delegates were reluctant to sever all ties with England. These conservatives were still loyal to the king despite their grievances with Parliament. In July, the delegates reached a compromise and voted to petition the king to free the colonies from troubles caused by Parliament. The delegates prepared a document that claimed that the tyranny of Parliament had left the congress no choice but to take up arms to protect their property,

A Letter from John Adams

Both a patriot leader and a future U.S. president, John Adams often confided to his wife Abigail his impressions of the great events he experienced. The following is part of a letter that is found in *Letters of Delegates to Congress* at the Library of Congress. In this letter, Adams described the creation of the Continental army, including the choice of its leader:

> *I can now inform you that the Congress have made Choice of the modest and virtuous, the amiable, generous and brave George Washington Esqr., to be the General of the American Army, and that he is to repair as soon as possible to the Camp before Boston. This Appointment will have a great Effect, in cementing and securing the Union of these Colonies. The Continent is really in earnest in defending the Country. They have voted Ten Companies of Rifle Men to be sent from Pennsylvania, Maryland and Virginia, to join the Army before Boston. These are an excellent Species of Light Infantry. They use a peculiar Kind of … Rifle—it has … Grooves within the Barrell, and carries [fires] a Ball, with great Exactness to great Distances. They are the most accurate Marksmen in the World. I begin to hope We shall not sit all Summer. I hope the People of our Province, will treat the General with all that Confidence and Affection, that Politeness and Respect, which is due to one of the most important Characters in the World. The Liberties of America, depend upon him, in a great Degree …*
>
> *It is long since I heard from you. I fear you have been kept in continual Alarms. My Duty and Love to all.*[1]

1. "John Adams to Abigail Adams, June 17 [1775]," *Letters of Delegates to Congress 1774–1789*, vol. 1, August 1774–August 1775, p. 498.

a move that Americans would willingly put aside once their rights were recognized: "[W]e mean not to dissolve that union which has so long and so happily subsisted between us, and which we sincerely wish to see restored."[18] This document—known as the Olive Branch Petition—was a final effort to avoid a full-scale war for independence.

George III and North, however, were unmoved; they saw only treason at work in the colonies and dispatched more troops to America to crush the rebels. In addition, Parliament cut off all trade with the colonies and authorized British vessels to intercept American merchant ships and search them for contraband.

Meanwhile, the fighting spread. In June, British soldiers under General William Howe drove armed militiamen from Breed's Hill near Boston but suffered a large number of casualties. Next, American troops moved into Canada. Led by General Richard Montgomery and Colonel Benedict Arnold, the patriots—as the American fighters were now called—captured Montreal but failed to occupy Quebec due to the effects of smallpox, hunger, and freezing weather. Making matters worse was Canada's failure to accept an American invitation to fight the British.

During the next few months, the Continental Congress established the first American navy. A boost in American morale came when the cannons from Fort Ticonderoga helped force the evacuation of the British from Boston on March 17, 1776. Three months later, British warships were turned back when they tried to take Charleston, South Carolina. The fighting showed no signs of stopping as the summer of 1776 began.

The Spirit of Independence Spreads

By 1776, a growing number of Americans, including many who had previously opposed going to war to form their own country, supported the call for independence. Colonists were inspired by the arguments in a popular new pamphlet called *Common Sense* that first appeared in January 1776. The author was Thomas Paine, a young Englishman who, despite having lived in America for less than two years, ardently championed the American cause. Using fiery, passionate, and compelling words, Paine implored readers to reject a king willing to ignore their rights and even kill them. He asserted that England was no longer fit to govern America. "There is something absurd in supposing a continent to be perpetually governed by an island,"[19]

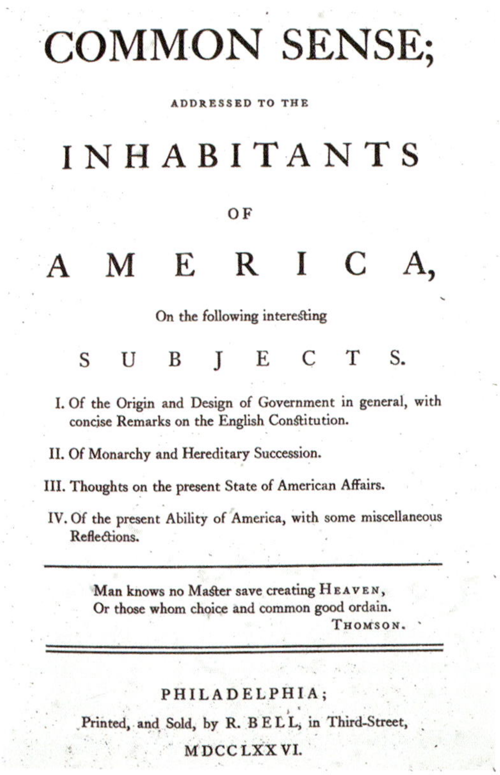

COMMON SENSE;

ADDRESSED TO THE

INHABITANTS

OF

AMERICA,

On the following interesting

SUBJECTS.

I. Of the Origin and Design of Government in general, with concise Remarks on the English Constitution.

II. Of Monarchy and Hereditary Succession.

III. Thoughts on the present State of American Affairs.

IV. Of the present Ability of America, with some miscellaneous Reflections.

Man knows no Master save creating Heaven,
Or those whom choice and common good ordain.
Thomson.

PHILADELPHIA;
Printed, and Sold, by R. BELL, in Third-Street,
MDCCLXXVI.

Shown here is the title page of Thomas Paine's Common Sense.

Paine Uses His Common Sense

Few documents inspired Americans to fight for independence as much as Thomas Paine's *Common Sense*. The following segment, which comes from Part III of the publication, focuses on Paine's concluding reasons why America should separate from Great Britain:

> *[The] most powerful of all arguments is, that nothing but independence, i.e. a continental form of government, can keep the peace of the continent and preserve it inviolate [secure] from civil wars. I dread the event of a reconciliation [compromise] with Britain now, as it is more than probable that it will be followed by a revolt somewhere or other, the consequences of which may be far more fatal than all the malice of Britain.*

> *[T]he general temper of the colonies towards a British government will be like that of a youth who is nearly out of his time; they will care very little about her. And a government which cannot preserve the peace is no government at all, and in that case we pay our money for nothing; and pray what is it that Britain can do, whose power will be wholly on paper, should a civil tumult break out the very day after reconciliation? I have heard some men say, many of whom I believe spoke without thinking, that they dreaded an independence, fearing that it would produce civil wars. It is but seldom that our first thoughts are truly correct, and that is the case here; for there is ten times more to dread from a patched up connection than from independence. I make the sufferer's case my own, and I protest, that were I driven from house and home, my property destroyed, and my circumstances ruined, that as a man, sensible of injuries, I could never relish the doctrine of reconciliation, or consider myself bound thereby.*[1]

Paine believed that it would be much more dangerous for Americans to try to reconcile with Britain. In his eyes, a clean break with Britain to form a new nation was the only option available to the Americans. Because of his strong, persuasive language, the independence movement grew stronger.

1. Quoted in Sculley Bradley et. al, eds., *The American Tradition in Literature*. New York, NY: Norton, 1967, pp. 293–294.

Paine wrote. Americans, he insisted, should fight for their independence, which was an idea that was sweeping across the colonies like wildfire.

Paine's words proved intoxicating to Americans at all levels. John Adams, a leading patriot and a future U.S. president, observed that "History will ascribe the [American] Revolution to Thomas Paine … Without the pen of Paine, the sword of Washington would have been wielded in vain."[20]

As the battle cry of freedom spread through the colonies, any hopes of reconciliation with England disappeared as the Second Continental Congress met. Almost all its members agreed with Richard Henry Lee of the Virginia delegation, who on June 7, 1776, stated, "These united colonies are, and ought to be, free and independent states."[21] Lee proposed a resolution to formally declare independence, establish foreign alliances, and create a plan for a government for the new nation. The first part of the resolution that was addressed was the call for independence.

Writing the Declaration of Independence

Delegates chose a committee to put Lee's ideas into writing. The man selected by the committee to write the first draft of the document was Thomas Jefferson of Virginia—a farmer, scholar, writer, and proponent of independence.

Jefferson wondered aloud why he was picked, but John Adams replied, "Reason first, you are a Virginian, and a Virginian ought to appear at the head of this business. Reason second, I am obnoxious, suspected, and unpopular. You are very much otherwise. Reason third, you can write ten times better than I can."[22]

With editing help from Franklin and Adams, Jefferson produced the Declaration of Independence, the world-famous document that artfully expressed many ideas inspired by the Enlightenment, particularly those initially penned by English philosopher John Locke. Neither a law nor constitution, the declaration was instead an open letter that proclaimed the radical idea that a just government depended on the consent of the governed. Moreover, it vowed "All men are created equal" and "endowed by their Creator with certain unalienable rights." When a government no longer served the needs of the people, Jefferson wrote, those same people had a right to abolish the government and establish a new one. In addition, the declaration contained a long list of grievances against the king, explaining why the Americans wanted to cut ties with the British and govern their own nation.

Officially Independent

On July 2, 1776, the delegates to the Second Continental Congress officially voted to declare independence from Britain. On July 4, they officially adopted the Declaration of Independence, though individual members signed it over a period of months. Such a move made clear to the world what the patriots wanted. It also provided the colonies with an unmistakable purpose to guide them through the dark days ahead. Washington's troops were no longer fighting to preserve their rights as Englishmen; they were fighting

The Declaration of Independence, shown here, is considered one of the most important documents in the history of American democracy.

for independence. To British loyalists, such a break was treasonous and punishable by death, a sentiment those at the signing of the Declaration of Independence understood. John Hancock of Massachusetts urged all delegates to write their names on the dangerous document to express unity. "We must hang together,"[23] he said. Reportedly, Franklin replied, "Yes, we must all hang together, or most assuredly, we shall all hang separately."[24]

By the next day, horseback riders headed out to deliver copies of the Declaration of Independence. When the document was read aloud to a public gathering in Philadelphia, militiamen and townspeople cheered. Some patriots even knocked down a statue of King George III in New York City after a reading of the declaration.

The Continental Army

Although the Continental army now had a clear cause to fight for, it had few resources. Its volunteer soldiers lacked discipline, organization, and a sense of military tradition. Life was hard and dangerous for these soldiers. Disease, infection, hunger, boredom, isolation, and exposure to the elements were the soldiers' constant companions. Lack of support from their fellow Americans was another problem. Even the Continental Congress did not always support them, as George Washington found out when he had to beg for money and supplies for his troops. Low pay and no compensation for war injuries undermined the morale of the American fighting force.

Patriot soldiers faced a professional army of British Regulars and German mercenaries, backed by the most powerful empire on earth. Unlike the Americans,the British troops were experienced and well supplied.

The colonists, however, enjoyed a few advantages. Although their militias were spread out over vast areas, the American fighters knew the terrain they fought upon. Americans also had a long tradition of bearing arms and defending themselves from Native Americans and other enemies. Drawing upon these experiences, they waged guerrilla war upon the

Tending to the Wounded

Some people believe the signers of the Declaration of Independence spent their time locked away in a room in Philadelphia. However, some of them had first-hand experience with the horrors of the fight for freedom. In the following passage from David McCullough's book *1776*, Dr. Benjamin Rush, a signer of the Declaration of Independence, describes his shock at his first glimpse of the gore of war:

> *The American army retired and left the British in possession of Trenton. The scene which accompanied and followed this combat was new to me. The first wounded man that came off the field was a New England soldier. His right hand hung a little above his wrist by nothing but a piece of skin. It had been broken by a cannon ball. I took charge of him and directed him to a house on the river which had been appropriated for a hospital. In the evening all the wounded, about 20 in number, were brought to this hospital and dressed by Dr. [John] Cochran, myself, and several young surgeons who acted under our direction. We all lay down on some straw in the same room with our wounded patients. It was now for the first time war appeared to me in its awful plenitude of horrors. I [lack] words to describe the anguish of my soul, excited by the cries and groans and convulsions of the men who lay by my side.*[1]

1. Quoted in David McCullough, *1776*. New York, NY: Simon & Schuster, 2005, p. 287.

British, engaging in a hit-and-run style of fighting that was difficult for the British to prepare for. Several highly competent officers also commanded the American troops. The greatest of them was Washington, who commanded respect from most revolutionary-era Americans. Finally, American soldiers now had a government—though a deeply flawed one—that legitimized their grievances against the king and compellingly argued that they had a legal right to resist British tyranny.

Britain Divided

Many people in Britain, including several members in Parliament, sympathized with the American cause and opposed the use of violence against them. Some believed the Americans were at war with the king and the British government, not the British people. Others were convinced the war in America was futile and would end disastrously for Britain. An ailing British statesman, William Pitt, warned Parliament in 1777, "You may ravage—you cannot conquer; it is impossible; you cannot conquer the Americans; I might as well talk of driving them before me with this crutch."[25]

Many nobles also opposed the king's war efforts. Even before the fighting in America had begun, these aristocrats were at odds with George III's attempts to revive the power of the monarchy that had been weakened in previous years. Though the nobility had few issues with exploiting the colonies themselves, they did not want the king to strengthen his position as a war leader at their own political expense. The mounting domestic opposition to the war led to the use of the German mercenaries called Hessians when the king was unable to enlist enough British soldiers to fight.

Retreating and Attacking

Such concerns, however, did not curb the king's desire to fight the Americans. In response to the Declaration of Independence, North, acting on the king's behalf, escalated the war by dispatching tens of thousands of British troops and Hessians to America. A large British fleet soon appeared in New York Harbor. By September, having endured fierce fighting, the patriots evacuated and were chased across Manhattan. Two months later, Washington's forces retreated across New Jersey, pursued by redcoats.

Washington's troops had crossed the Delaware River into Pennsylvania, destroying bridges behind them. Safely camped on the other side, they waited as winter settled in. The situation was grim for the Americans. Washington's forces numbered fewer than 10,000—all of them hungry, cold, dejected, and dressed in rags. By winter 1776, almost three-fourths of them were on the verge of completing their enlistments and being eligible to go home. Faced with this reality, Washington decided to use his troops while he still had men to command.

On the night of December 25, 1776, Washington and his troops huddled in small boats as they crossed the Delaware River in freezing rain. Just before dawn on December 26, they attacked sleeping Hessian troops in Trenton, New Jersey, capturing around 900 soldiers.

Buoyed by this major success, many of Washington's men stayed with the general as he led another attack against British redcoats at Princeton a week later, forcing them to retreat to New Brunswick, Canada. Afterward, the fatigued Americans settled in at Morristown and waited for spring.

Saratoga and Its Aftermath

Warm weather brought renewed fighting, and in September 1777, Howe's forces fended off attacks from Washington's men and captured Philadelphia, a patriot stronghold. Howe was triumphant again a week later at Germanton when his men repelled another attack from Washington.

Things ended badly, however, for another British commander, General John Burgoyne, who led more than

The Battle of Saratoga is considered one of the turning points in the American Revolution.

7,000 men from Canada to take control of the Hudson River in New York. However, Burgoyne underestimated the tenacity of the patriots waiting for him at Freeman's Farm near Saratoga, New York. American forces led by Horatio Gates and Benedict Arnold overwhelmed Burgoyne's army, forcing his surrender on October 17, 1777.

This American victory proved to be a turning point in the war. For one thing, American morale soared when the colonists discovered that they could defeat and capture a British army. It also gave French leaders the confidence they needed to openly and fully support the American war effort. France, which was an old enemy of England, had unofficially supplied the Americans with military and financial help during much of the war, but it had wavered in lending its full support. After the American triumph at Saratoga, however, French leaders believed that America could win the war, costing England its American colonies. Because a weakened England was in France's best interest, the French king agreed in February 1778 to make an official military alliance with the Americans and declared

The Brutal Winter at Valley Forge

During the winter of 1777, the American forces camped at Valley Forge in Pennsylvania. There, they struggled through the long winter and difficult periods of sickness and starvation. A French volunteer known as the Chevalier de Pontgibaud traveled to the American encampment at Valley Forge. In the following passage, he describes the wretched conditions he found there:

> *Soon I came in sight of the camp. My imagination had pictured an army with uniforms, the glitter of arms standards, etc., in short, military pomp of all sorts. Instead … I saw, grouped together or standing alone, a few militiamen, poorly clad, and for the most part without shoes—many of them badly armed, but all well supplied with provisions … In passing through the camp I also noticed soldiers wearing cotton nightcaps under their hats, and some having for cloaks or greatcoats, coarse woolen blankets, exactly like those provided for the patients in our French hospitals. I learned afterwards that these were the officers and generals.*
>
> *Such, in strict truth was, at the time I came amongst them the appearance of this armed mob, the leader of whom was the man who has rendered the name of Washington famous; such were the colonists—unskilled warriors who learned in a few years how to conquer the finest troops that England could send against them.*[1]

1. Quoted in Stephen Ambrose and Douglas Brinkley, *Witness to America: An Illustrated Documentary History of the United States from the Revolution to Today*. New York, NY: HarperCollins, 1999, pp. 20–21.

war against England. For the first time, a foreign power had recognized America as an independent nation. Spain joined France in declaring war on Britain a year later.

Despite a huge influx of much-needed money, weapons, ships, and manpower from France, the war was far from over. Fighting in America continued for years after Saratoga, in part because British General Henry Clinton began to concentrate on the South. There, the British expected to find strong pockets of loyalists who would rush to aid England. By the end of 1778, the British had taken Savannah, Georgia, and soon controlled all of that state.

The redcoats then attacked Charleston,

South Carolina. After months of fighting, the South's most important city surrendered in May 1780.

Victory at Yorktown

The next big campaign took place when British general Charles Cornwallis successfully led his troops into the hills of South Carolina and beat the Americans at the Battle of Camden. From there, his men battled their way through North Carolina and into Yorktown, Virginia, where his forces built fortifications along the seacoast and waited for British warships to provide military support. Soon afterward, Washington launched a surprise attack against Cornwallis at Yorktown.

As Washington's troops advanced, a French fleet occupied the Chesapeake River and blocked British ships, thus cutting off supplies to Cornwallis's men and taking away their means of escape. On October 17, 1781, a battered and out-maneuvered Cornwallis had no choice but to hoist up the white flag of surrender. Two days later, as the British military band played "The

This engraving shows the British surrender to Washington's forces at Yorktown.

World Turned Upside Down," American troops took control of Cornwallis's forces, and the British marched out of Yorktown. Though a few smaller battles continued after Cornwallis's surrender, the war in America was essentially over. It would take another two years, however, for what had grown into a global conflict to officially end.

Peace in the New Nation

England's defeat in the American Revolution caused the fall of North and his ministers, who were replaced by new officials more sympathetic to the American cause. A peace treaty, however, was delayed because France was still at war with England. Under their alliance with France, the Americans could negotiate with Britain separately from France, but they could not come to a separate peace.

Under the terms of the Treaty of Paris, which was signed in September 1783, George III recognized American independence. The treaty also established that America's boundaries ranged from the Atlantic Ocean to the Mississippi River and from the Great Lakes to Florida. It lifted any British barrier to Americans wanting to navigate the Mississippi and fish off the coast of Newfoundland. In addition, the British agreed to remove their troops from the new nation as soon as they were able. For their part, American officials

The new nation that emerged after the American Revolution—officially known as the United States of America—even had its own flag. It had 13 stars to represent the 13 states. The Continental Congress officially adopted this flag in 1777.

promised to urge the states to compensate British loyalists for any confiscated property and to try to remove any legal obstacles to the collection of prewar debts owed to businessmen in England.

At last, Americans had achieved independence and recognition as a sovereign nation. War had bound the nation together. Now, however, the nation's leaders faced the daunting task of creating a government that could hold the new nation together during a time of peace.

Chapter Four

GOVERNING THE NEW NATION

During the American Revolution, the new nation had been united under a constitution known as the Articles of Confederation. This document, which established a loose confederation of states under a fairly weak central government, was adopted by the Continental Congress in 1777, but it took until 1781 for it to be ratified by all the states. The Articles of Confederation were a product of their time, giving most of the power to the states out of fear of a tyrannical central government such as the British monarchy they were fighting in the war.

The Articles reflected the American mindset at the time they were written, but by the time the war ended in 1783, things had already changed. The national government and state governments were in debt, American cities needed to be rebuilt, and veterans suffered from physical and mental trauma following their service in the war. As Americans continued to carve out their own national identity, they struggled under a governing system that was not strong enough for the challenges they were facing.

The Idea of Equality

Americans cared deeply about how they should be governed in the years following the war. Their political senses had been stirred by the American Revolution. Now freed of British control, Americans asserted their rights, freedoms, goals, and interests. The country was suddenly swept up by the ideals of democracy and equality, as people celebrated the words of the Declaration of Independence: "All men are created equal." The opposition to royalty and privileged classes that developed during the revolutionary period now lingered after the war. State governments also contributed to the trend by outlawing titles of nobility from foreign countries.

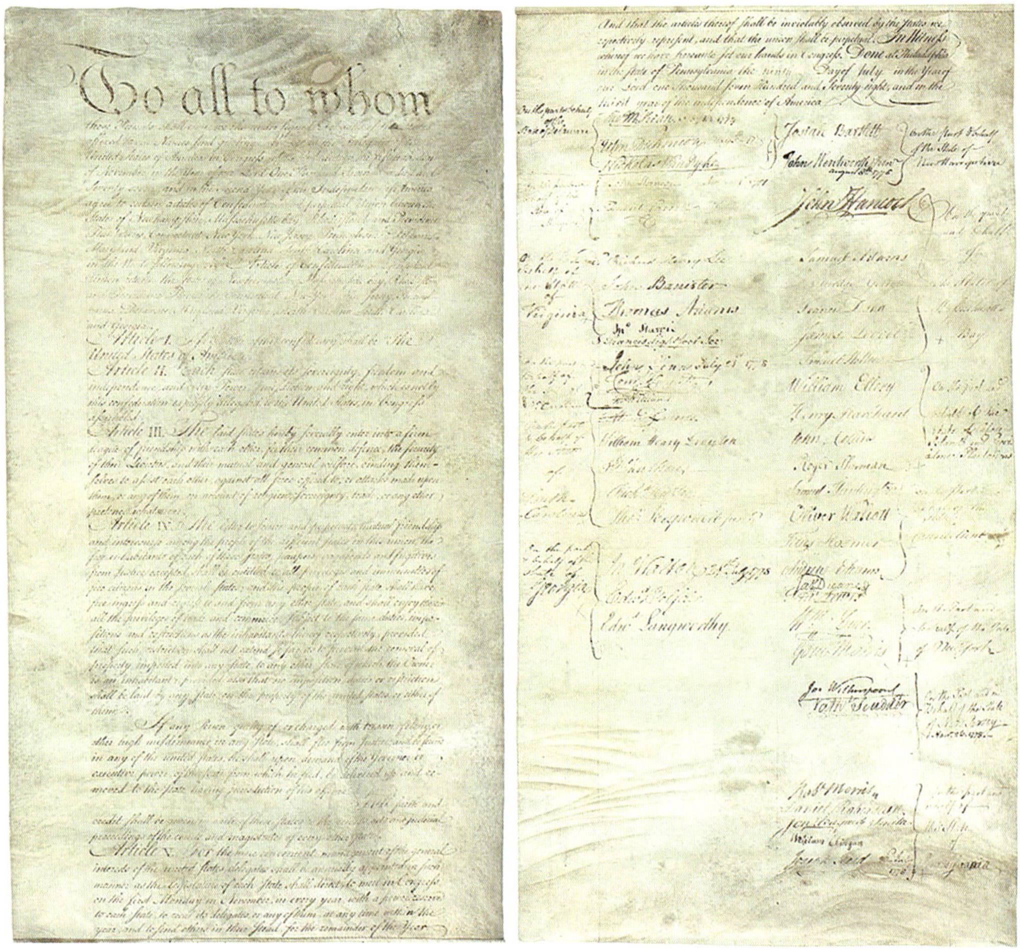
To all to whom

The Articles of Confederation, shown here, formed the backbone of American government in the years immediately following the American Revolution. This document was the young nation's first attempt at creating a national constitution.

The economic impact of war also helped to level the economic difference between America's social classes. In many cases, wealthy merchants suffered financial loss when fighting destroyed their businesses. Others suffered when British blockades prevented American ships from carrying cargo to markets. Farmers, however, often saw their fortunes rise by selling vegetables and grain to the military. Meanwhile, state governments confiscated and auctioned the properties of wealthy loyalists who had been driven out of America to live in Canada, the West Indies, or England. Though speculators bought many of these estates, they often sold them as small and affordable parcels of land, enabling many Americans to own property for the first time.

However, there were still many

How Did the Revolution Change America?

David Ramsay, a South Carolina physician and witness to the American Revolution, observed in his *History of the American Revolution*, published in 1789, how the war had changed American society:

> *The Americans knew but little of one another previous to the Revolution. Trade and business had brought the inhabitants of their seaports acquainted with each other, but the bulk of the people in the interior country were unacquainted with their fellow citizens. A Continental army and Congress composed of men from all the states, by freely mixing together, were assimilated into one mass. Individuals of both, mingling with the citizens, disseminated [communicated] principles of union [ideas for national unity] among them. Local prejudices abated [lessened] …*
>
> *Intermarriages of different states were much more common than before the war and became an additional cement to the Union. Unreasonable jealousies had existed between the inhabitants of the Eastern and of the Southern states, but on becoming better acquainted with each other, these in a great measure subsided …*
>
> *Religious bigotry had broken in upon the peace of various sects before the American war. This was kept up by partial establishments, and by a dread that the Church of England … would … triumph over all other denominations. These apprehensions [worries] were done away by the Revolution.*[1]

1. Quoted in Stephen Ambrose and Douglas Brinkley, *Witness to America: An Illustrated Documentary History of the United States from the Revolution to Today*. New York, NY: HarperCollins, 1999, p. 25.

instances in which this era's definition of equality differed greatly from how it is defined in America today. Voting rights were often granted only to white landowners. Women were still considered inferior to men and could not vote, and slavery was still practiced throughout the country.

Equality and Slavery

This new interest in the concept of equality forced Americans to reconsider slavery.

During the American Revolution, thousands of blacks had fought alongside both the Americans and the British with hopes of being rewarded with freedom. At the end of the war, great numbers departed on British ships to live as free people abroad. Others were left behind and returned to slavery. Now, however, these individuals wanted the rights implied in the Declaration of Independence. In 1780, seven black men caught up in the new spirit of equality petitioned the state government of Massachusetts for the right to vote. Following the example set by American revolutionaries, they argued that taxation without representation for black people living in the United States was unjust: "We … [are distressed] … that while we are not allowed the Privilage of freemen of the State having no vote or Influence in the Election of those that Tax us yet many of our Colour (as is well known) have cheerfully Entered the field of Battle in the defense of the Common Cause [the American Revolution] and … [against England's unfair system of taxation]."[26] Three years later, voting rights were granted to black men in Massachusetts who paid their taxes.

Though some Americans, including Southerners, freed their slaves and Northern states began abolishing slavery not long after the war ended, the entire country was not yet ready for the emancipation of all slaves. In the Deep South, in fact, the institution of slavery continued for another eight decades until the nation erupted in civil war.

Problems with the Articles

Governing the new nation was the most pressing problem faced by Americans.

The institution of slavery went against the idea that "all men are created equal."

This became increasingly clear as the spirit of wartime unity faded. For many Americans, the war deepened their love of their state rather than their love for their nation.

Overseas, meanwhile, watchful British observers doubted America's ability to become a successful sovereign nation. In fact, because many royal authorities expected the American experiment in self-government to fail, they scorned attempts by their former colonies to negotiate fair trade practices. Josiah Tucker, dean of England's Gloucester Cathedral, predicted of the former colonists, "A disunited people till the end of time, suspicious and distrustful of each other, they will be divided and subdivided into little commonwealths or principalities, according to natural boundaries."[27]

Tucker's vision of a divided America, however, proved false—at least as far as individual states were concerned. American state governments, in fact, were managing to govern themselves in the wake of the British departure. State constitutions, bills of rights, and republics created during the American Revolution still functioned effectively.

Trouble mounted, however, at the national level. There, America headed toward disunity, as Tucker predicted. Much of the problem lay with the Articles of Confederation, which called for a "league of friendship" between the former colonies. It was now clear, though, that under this loose federation the states acted as separate republics rather than as one nation. They bickered over taxes and tariffs. New York, for instance, taxed firewood from Connecticut and dairy products from New Jersey. States also imposed taxes on foreign goods crossing their borders from other states.

Boundary disputes also strained relations between states. According to their charters, Georgia, Virginia, North Carolina, South Carolina, Connecticut, and Massachusetts could claim territorial western boundaries that reached the Pacific Ocean. All too often, these claims conflicted and resulted in violence. Pennsylvania and Virginia came to blows over land in the area around present-day Pittsburgh, while settlers in what is now Kentucky threatened to use violence to break away from Virginia. Meanwhile, the remaining states with territorial boundaries that were fixed by the sea or their neighboring states wanted the federal government to take charge of the western territories, make them possessions of the entire nation, and set up rules for statehood.

Though the western boundary issue was ultimately settled by the federal government through the Northwest Ordinance of 1787, other legal problems proved harder, if not impossible, to fix. No longer could states take interstate disputes to British judges. Not much help came from the national government because the Articles of Confederation allowed for no federal judiciary branch. It also did not provide for a permanent executive branch of government.

The Articles of Confederation had

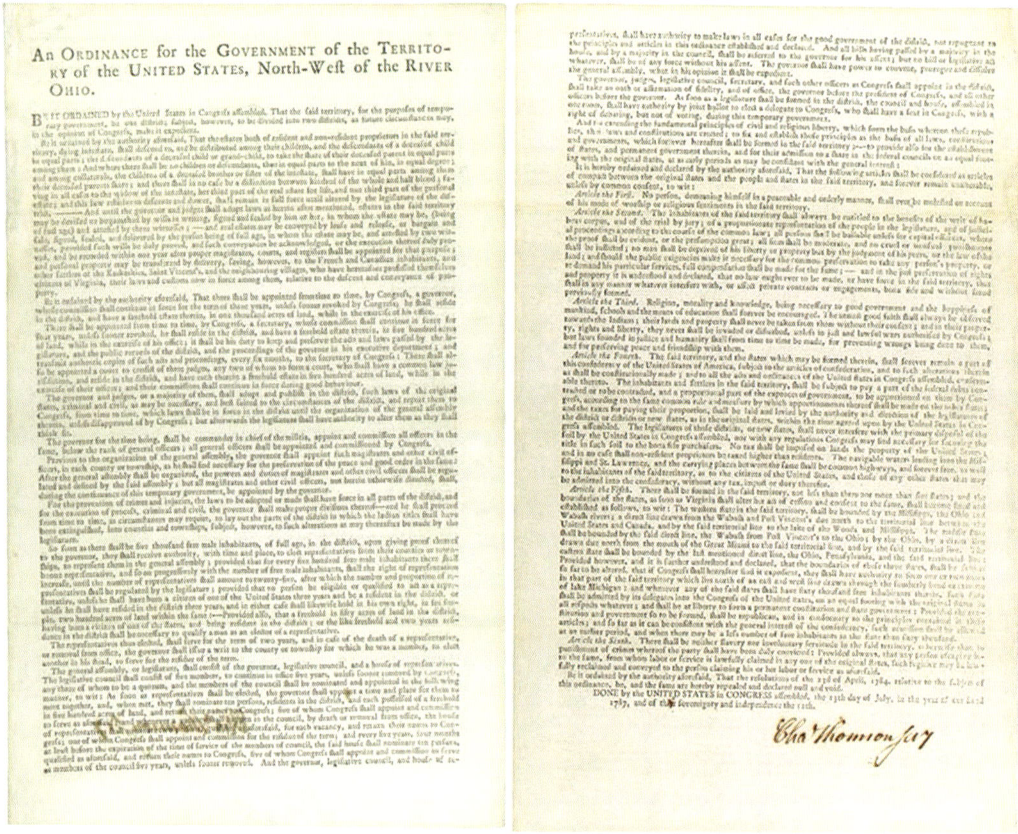

An ORDINANCE for the GOVERNMENT of the TERRITORY of the UNITED STATES, North-West of the RIVER OHIO.

The Northwest Ordinance, shown here, is considered one of the few successes of the federal government under the Articles of Confederation. It allowed for the creation of new western states, established the guidelines for statehood, and contained a bill of rights for those living in western territories.

many other flaws. Under its provisions, each state had one vote to cast for laws, regardless of the size of its population. Congress was crippled by a provision that some important bills, such as those having to do with treaties and money, required approval from nine of the thirteen states to pass. Because of this rule, a significant piece of legislation could be defeated even though most delegates supported it.

Congress was also unable to regulate commerce or impose taxes. Nor could it force states to provide funds to pay the cost of maintaining the nation. As a result, many states refused to pay their share, angering those states that did. Meanwhile, the national debt grew larger. Other money matters added to the nation's problems. Each state, for example, coined its own money and printed paper money that inflated the

Jefferson's Concerns

In a February 15, 1783, letter to fellow Virginian Edmund Randolph, Thomas Jefferson confessed his concern that the new American republic may be headed to war:

> *I find also the pride of [independence] taking deep and dangerous hold on the hearts of individual states. I know no danger so dreadful and so probable as that of internal contests. And I know no remedy so likely to prevent it as the strengthening the band that connects us. We have substituted a Congress of deputies from every state to perform this task; but we have done nothing which would enable them to enforce their decisions. What will be the case? They will not be enforced. The states will go to war with each other in defiance of Congress; one will call in France to her assistance; and Great Britain, and so we shall have all the wars of Europe brought to our own doors.*[1]

Jefferson feared that the weak national government set up by the Articles of Confederation would be unable to stop states that were in conflict from going to war to settle their disputes. He believed only a stronger sense of national unity—and a stronger national government—could enforce the laws necessary to avoid another war.

1. Quoted in John M. Blum, William S. McFeely, Edmund S. Morgan, Arthur M. Schlesinger Jr., Kenneth M. Stampp, and C. Vann Woodward, *The National Experience: A History of the United States*, 6th ed. San Diego, CA: Harcourt Brace Jovanovich, 1985, p. 132.

money supply. Under the Articles of Confederation, the federal government had no way to control this.

A Struggling Nation

As the national government struggled, some Americans feared that states might even fight among themselves, break away from the confederacy, and form alliances with Spain, France, or England. A few conservative Americans called for a monarchy or military rule to keep order in the states.

Trouble also loomed beyond the western borders of the United States. Spain, for example, refused to let Americans navigate the Mississippi and ship their products and goods to sea unless they paid export fees in New Orleans. British troops, meanwhile, remained in North America, refusing to leave the western frontier until Americans honored the peace treaty and paid their debts to England. Some state governments, however, complicated matters by passing laws to create obstacles to collecting these debts.

Meanwhile, American settlers who felt threatened by Native Americans in the Ohio River Valley demanded military protection. Raising funds to strengthen the army was hard to do, given that the federal government had not yet paid many of the soldiers who had fought in the Revolution. In addition, the army was becoming even more undisciplined and demoralized.

Tensions Lead to Rebellion

A postwar period of economic hardship added to the problems the new nation was facing. A key issue was that America's staggering war debts had to be paid, but revenues had been reduced because trade with England had been cut off during the war. Although America again traded with its former enemy after the war, the new nation now imported more than it exported. This trade imbalance resulted in vast amounts of silver and gold being sent from America to England. Making matters worse, some states continued issuing paper money to pay off their debts, even though there was no gold in their treasuries to back the currency.

Farmers were hit especially hard. Their failure to make debt payments or pay taxes resulted in foreclosures that forced them off their farms. Some even ended up in debtors' prisons. Pure desperation drove many farmers to demand that their state legislatures enact laws that delayed or eased their debt payments. Lawmakers, however, routinely rejected these requests. In Massachusetts, many farmers were infuriated that the merchants who seized farmlands for debt failures were often members of the state legislature that denied their requests for help. Adding insult to injury, farmers lost the right to vote when their property was taken.

Tensions finally exploded when Daniel Shays, a farmer and veteran of the American Revolution, led 1,200 angry farmers in armed rebellion in Massachusetts. Shays's men halted auctions of bankrupted farms, disrupted court proceedings, and, in some cases, robbed wealthy businessmen. They also had plans to take control of a store of muskets at a Springfield arsenal.

Although state militia troops suppressed the uprising, Shays's Rebellion sent shock waves throughout the 13 states and caused many to wonder if another revolution was brewing, especially with a central government that did not have the power to put down any such uprisings. Washington wrote, "I predict the worst consequences for a half-starved, limping government, always moving upon crutches and tottering at every step … I do not conceive we can exist long as a nation without having lodged somewhere a power which will pervade the whole Union."[28] Shays's Rebellion was a turning point in the quest to create a successful government for the United States. It proved to Americans that things needed to change.

Shays's Rebellion occurred in response to high taxes and other economic strains, including the fact that veterans such as Shays had not been paid for their military service.

Calling for a Convention

Across the nation, many powerful leaders agreed that something needed to be done to strengthen the central government if America was to survive as a nation. New York's Alexander Hamilton—a brilliant politician who had once served as Washington's aide-de-camp, or assistant, and an outspoken advocate of a strong national government—complained, "The confederation itself is defective and requires to be altered; it is neither fit for

Hamilton Speaks Out

Alexander Hamilton, statesman and a veteran of the American Revolution, was a supporter of a strong national government and an early critic of the Articles of Confederation. This excerpt from his September 3, 1780, letter to James Duane, a New York delegate to Congress, shows his worry that the Articles of Confederation did not provide a strong army, which he saw as necessary for the unity and defense of the nation:

> *The fundamental defect is a want [lack] of power in Congress. It is hardly worth while to show in what this consists, as it seems to be universally acknowledged, or to point to how it has happened, as the only question is how to remedy it … The entire formation and disposal of our military forces ought to belong to Congress. It is an essential cement of the union; and it ought to be the policy of Congress to destroy all ideas of state attachment in the army and make it look up wholly to them … Already some of the lines of the army would obey their states in opposition to Congress … Without a speedy change the army must dissolve; it is now a mob, rather than an army, without clothing, without pay, without provision, without morals, without discipline.*[1]

1. Quoted in Richard Haesly, ed., *The Constitutional Convention*. San Diego, CA: Greenhaven, 2002, pp. 44–47.

Alexander Hamilton

war, nor peace."[29]

James Madison, a congressman from Virginia, also recognized the need for correcting weaknesses in the national government. He brought his concerns to a meeting at Annapolis, Maryland, initially set up to discuss navigation problems Virginia and Maryland were having on the

The meetings of the Constitutional Convention took place in the Pennsylvania State House, which is now called Independence Hall.

Potomac River. There, Madison asked the delegates to consider bigger issues and proposed that they ask Congress to set up a national convention for the purpose of revising the Articles of Confederation.

A majority agreed with the idea and authorized the convention to begin in Philadelphia in May 1787. Franklin wrote to Jefferson, describing the importance of the upcoming convention, "Our federal constitution is generally thought defective, and a convention, first proposed by Virginia, and since recommended by Congress, is to assemble here next month, to revise it and propose amendments … If it does not do good it will do harm, as it will show that we have not the wisdom enough among us to govern ourselves."[30] It seemed the fate of American democracy was hanging in the balance when what we now call the Constitutional Convention began.

Though many Americans agreed that such a convention was necessary, they were at odds over what kinds of revisions they should make. Some wanted a large, powerful government to provide national security. Others, however, worried that such a government would threaten their liberties. Instead, they favored keeping state governments strong and independent. The delegates traveling to Philadelphia soon found out that addressing these opposite views would be a challenging balancing act.

Chapter Five

THE CONSTITUTIONAL CONVENTION

The meetings that we now know as the Constitutional Convention were attended by many prominent Americans. Although 74 men were originally selected as delegates to the convention, only 55 took part in the meetings. However, these 55 men were some of the brightest political visionaries of their time. Among them were Alexander Hamilton, a delegate from New York, and Benjamin Franklin, who came from Pennsylvania. George Washington, the hero of the American Revolution, was also present at the convention despite his reluctance to leave his family and farm. Another pair of famous names joined Washington as delegates from Virginia: George Mason, the primary author of the Virginia Declaration of Rights, and James Madison, who later became the fourth U.S. president.

Many delegates took long journeys in horse-drawn coaches to reach Philadelphia. They traveled to the city from every state except Rhode Island. They often traveled with their wives and children, settling in for the duration of the convention at hotels, lodges, and private homes in the city. One of the more popular places to stay was the Indian Queen, which was a tavern and hotel. Historian Charles L. Mee Jr. described this setting as a familiar one for American politicians:

> *The guests sat about in … chairs pulled up at large round tables, smoking long-stemmed clay pipes and drinking … lemonade laced with wine, bowls of punch, or Madeira, reading English and American papers and magazines, checking the notices and broadsides tacked up near the bar, exchanging news and gossip in what was still, as it had been for scores of years, the … natural setting for politics in America.*[31]

George Washington is shown here signing the Constitution.

The leaders who met to discuss news and politics in taverns such as the Indian Queen brought that same spirit of open discussion to the Constitutional Convention. Many of these men had already played some role in shaping America's independent identity. A majority had taken part in the Continental Congress, and several had helped create their state governments. A group of delegates had also fought in the American Revolution, and they brought their passion for liberty and desire to protect the ideals they fought for to Philadelphia.

More than 30 delegates were lawyers or had some form of legal training, but the rest of the delegates represented a wide range of trades—from merchants to plantation owners. They also represented a wide range of regional interests. Farmers from the South had different goals than lawyers from New York City, and these differences led to lively debates throughout the convention.

The delegates had different ideas about what was the best system of government for the young nation. However, they all seemed to agree that the Articles of Confederation did not set up the best system of government. Things needed to change, and it was their job to create a government that would best serve their fellow Americans.

Although the delegates represented different groups of Americans, they did not represent all Americans. They were all white men, which meant that the interests of other groups—women, slaves, free black Americans, and Native Americans among them—were not fully represented at the Constitutional Convention. As such, the document they created was not inclusive toward groups who were different from the men who drafted it. It took years—sometimes centuries—and many amendments before the Constitution

A First-Person Account of Alexander Hamilton

Thanks to the written observations of William Pierce, a Georgia delegate at the Constitutional Convention, modern readers are presented with colorful insights into some of the major participants in the debates that forged the U.S. Constitution. The following is Pierce's description of Alexander Hamilton:

> *Col. [Alexander] Hamilton is deservedly celebrated for his talents. He is a practitioner of the law, and reputed to be a finished scholar … it is my opinion that he is rather a convincing Speaker, than a blazing orator. Col. Hamilton requires time to think—he enquires into every part of his subject with the searchings of philosophy, and when he comes forward he comes highly charged with interesting matter; there is no skimming over the surface of a subject with him; he must sink to the bottom to see what foundation it rests on. His language is not always equal … he rambles just enough to strike and keep up the attention. He is about 33 years old, of small stature, and lean. His manners are tinctured [tinted] with stiffness, and sometimes with a degree of vanity that is highly disagreeable.*[1]

1. Quoted in Richard Haesly, ed., *The Constitutional Convention*. San Diego, CA: Greenhaven, 2002, pp. 80–81.

granted the same rights to all Americans that were initially granted only to those who looked like the men who wrote the document.

Who Did Not Attend?

Though many famous names in American politics were among the delegates assembled in Philadelphia, several of America's top leaders did not attend the convention. Thomas Jefferson and John Adams were serving as ambassadors in Europe, and John Jay, a respected statesman and a future chief justice of the U.S. Supreme Court, was in New York serving as the secretary for foreign affairs. Thomas Paine, whose words had meant so much during the American Revolution, was also in Europe on business.

Strong doubts, however, kept away the fiery speaker Patrick Henry. Though Henry was selected to represent Virginia, he refused the position. "I smelt a rat,"[32] he said, revealing his suspicion that the convention intended to overthrow the power of the states.

A Calm, Thoughtful Approach

Most of the delegates who made the trip to Philadelphia were scholars who understood the importance of the task at hand. They were influenced by the Enlightenment and used reason to guide their actions. These delegates believed a calm, thoughtful approach was the best way to restructure America's government.

One of these delegates was James Madison, who arrived weeks before the convention began. Months earlier, upon request, Jefferson had sent Madison hundreds of books on government, law, and philosophy to help Madison prepare his thoughts for the convention. For years Madison had believed the "league of friendship" between the 13 states had failed, and as he studied these books, he became convinced it was time for a new constitution.

James Madison spent a long time studying before the Constitutional Convention officially began. He wanted to learn as much as he could to help build the best government for the United States.

The First Plans Emerge

By May 25, 1787, enough delegates had arrived to get the convention underway at the Pennsylvania State House. One of the first items of business was to elect Washington to preside over the convention. George Wythe of Virginia presented the rules: Among other restrictions, delegates could not whisper, pass notes, or read books or newspapers when another was speaking. Each state was allowed to cast one vote regardless of how many delegates were present.

The delegates also adopted a procedure called the "Committee of the Whole." Under this informal system, members could debate issues as they would in one large committee rather than a formal legislative body; they could also vote but not be bound by their votes if they changed their minds as arguments unfolded. This was done to encourage open-minded thinking and discussion.

Several delegates kept notes during the proceedings, but Madison made the best and most complete notes that are still read today. He never missed a meeting.

Edmund Randolph, Virginia's governor and a delegate from that state, opened the convention to main business when he proposed a new constitution that he

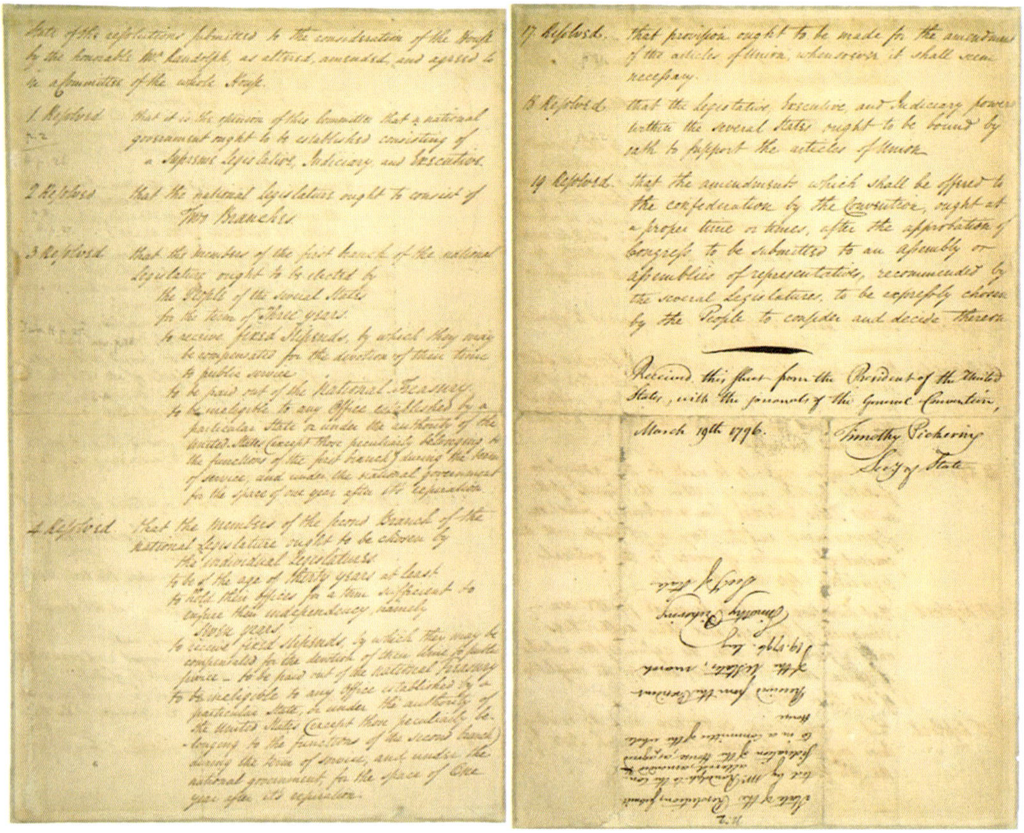
State of the resolutions submitted to the consideration of the House by the honorable Mr. Randolph, as altered, amended, and agreed to in a Committee of the whole House.

1 Resolved that it is the opinion of this Committee that a national government ought to be established consisting of a Supreme Legislative, Judiciary, and Executive.

2 Resolved that the national legislature ought to consist of Two Branches

3 Resolved that the members of the first branch of the national Legislature ought to be elected by the People of the several States for the term of Three years. to receive fixed stipends, by which they may be compensated for the devotion of their time to public service to be paid out of the National Treasury. to be ineligible to any Office established by a particular State or under the authority of the United States (except those peculiarly belonging to the functions of the first branch) during the term of service, and under the national government for the space of one year after its expiration.

4 Resolved that the members of the second Branch of the national Legislature ought to be chosen by the individual Legislatures. to be of the age of thirty years at least. to hold their offices for a term sufficient to ensure their independency, namely seven years. to receive fixed stipends, by which they may be compensated for the devotion of their time to public service – to be paid out of the national Treasury. to be ineligible to any office established by a particular State, or under the authority of the United States (except those peculiarly belonging to the functions of the second branch) during the term of service, and under the national government, for the space of One year after its expiration.

17 Resolved. that provision ought to be made for the amendment of the articles of Union, whensoever it shall seem necessary.

18 Resolved that the Legislative, Executive, and Judiciary powers within the several States ought to be bound by oath to support the articles of Union

19 Resolved. that the amendments which shall be offered to the confederation by the Convention, ought at a proper time or times, after the approbation of Congress to be submitted to an assembly or assemblies of representatives, recommended by the several Legislatures, to be expressly chosen by the People to consider and decide thereon.

Received this sheet from the President of the United States, with the Journals of the General Convention, March 19th 1796. Timothy Pickering Secy of State

Shown here is the original text of the Virginia Plan.

and Madison had drafted. Their Virginia Plan called for a strong federal government made up of three branches—executive, judicial, and legislative. Each of these branches would be able to check, or balance, the power of the others. The national government could also veto, or reject, state laws.

Charles Pinckney, a 29-year-old South Carolina planter, offered another proposal. Because surviving documents are not clear as to what Pinckney presented that opening day, historians are not sure what his plan entailed. Pinckney claimed that his plan was the basis for what became the U.S. Constitution, but modern historians doubt this claim is true. Whatever Pinckney's plan was, the convention ignored it in favor of Madison and Randolph's plan. Their new constitution had become the central issue of debate.

Questioning the Virginia Plan

As the convention continued, the delegates agreed to keep their talks secret and not to discuss them outside the Pennsylvania State House. Sentries, or guards, were posted outside the door of the room where they met to keep out unauthorized people.

Ten days of debate followed, as delegates discussed many important questions posed by the Virginia Plan. What was meant by the phrase "the federal government"? Did "federal" mean "supreme," or did it suggest a compact among the states? Did the Virginia Plan intend to overthrow state governments?

Delegates also questioned whether the country needed a president—one who ran a separate branch of government and did not preside over the legislature. Some asserted that an individual with great powers was needed to protect the nation in a crisis. Others thought the country needed several executives. Critics, however, feared that such power, whether concentrated in the hands of one person or many, inevitably set the stage for dictatorship and tyranny. Some wanted to know how long a president's term of office should be.

At one point, Gouverneur Morris, a delegate from Pennsylvania, defended the call for a strong national government, saying it was necessary to ward off a worse form of government. "We had better take a supreme government now than a despot [dictator] twenty years hence—for come he must,"[33] Morris said.

In addition, delegates quarreled over details for a bicameral, or two-house, legislature. Under the Virginia Plan, the number of representatives for each house would be based on population, thus giving the advantage to more populated states. States with smaller populations did not agree with this proposal.

A Long, Hot Summer

As the debate wore on, delegates sweltered in the summer heat, which was made worse because all windows of the state house were closed to keep out the swarms of black flies that infested Philadelphia. Writer William K. Stevens described the conditions the delegates faced that summer: "Flies and mosquitoes added their torment to the oppressive heat of that summer, the worst in nearly 40 years."[34]

Enduring the heat and the flies, the delegates continued their deliberations. They agreed that three branches of government with a system of "checks and balances" were necessary to prevent one person or branch of government from obtaining too much power. However, they still could not come together on the issue of proportionate representation versus equal representation. Delegates from larger states favored the proportional approach, while those from smaller states generally called for equal representation.

The New Jersey Plan

By June 15, the convention took a new turn. William Paterson of New Jersey, frustrated with the Virginia Plan, presented his own plan to the convention. His plan called for a one-house legislature that allowed each state—big or small—

Rules for Debating

The following excerpt of the rules for discussion used by the delegates at the Constitutional Convention comes from *The Debates in the Several State Conventions on the Adoption of the Federal Constitution*, a five-volume collection compiled by Jonathan Elliot in the mid-19th century:

> *Every member, rising to speak, shall address the president; and, whilst he shall be speaking, none shall pass between them, or hold discourse with another, or read a book, pamphlet, or paper, printed or manuscript.*
>
> *And of two members rising at the same time, the president shall name him who shall be first heard.*
>
> *A member shall not speak oftener than twice, without special leave, upon the same question; and not the second time, before every other, who had been silent, shall have been heard, if he choose to speak upon the subject.*
>
> *A motion made and seconded shall be repeated, and if written, as it shall be when any member shall so require, read aloud, by the secretary, before it shall be debated; and may be withdrawn at any time before the vote upon it shall have been declared …*
>
> *A member may be called to order by any other member, as well as by the president, and may be allowed to explain his conduct, or expressions, supposed to be reprehensible [in the wrong]; and all questions of order shall be decided by the president, without appeal or debate …*
>
> *When the house shall adjourn, every member shall stand in his place until the president pass him.*[1]

1. Jonathan Elliot, *The Debates in the Several State Conventions on the Adoption of the Federal Constitution.* Philadelphia, PA: J. B. Lippincott, 1896.

one vote. As he spoke, delegates realized that the intent of this New Jersey Plan was for the nation to remain as a gathering of states with equal power. Paterson's plan, in effect, kept basic principles of the Articles of Confederation intact, except that Congress would have the power to tax and regulate foreign affairs.

The convention debated Paterson's proposal for three days and then rejected it. On June 18, Hamilton spent six hours offering yet another proposal, though it received no support. Among other things, critics disliked his call for an executive that would serve for life and have the power to veto all laws. To many, this sounded like a monarchy. Hamilton left the convention not long afterward.

Though the rival plans had been voted down, the representatives of the smaller states had clarified their unhappiness with the Virginia Plan. Some were so angry that they threatened to leave the convention unless provisions were made for at least one house based on population. Delaware's Gunning Bedford warned that if the larger states imposed a strong national government, "The small ones will find some foreign ally of more honor and good faith, who will take them by the hand and do them justice."[35]

Bedford's rash remarks sent shock waves throughout the convention. Other delegates quickly rebuked him. Rufus King from Massachusetts declared, "Whatever may be my distress I will never court a foreign power to assist in relieving myself from it."[36]

Sherman's Two-House Plan

Bitter debate—especially over the representation question—raged until the end of June. By that point, the debate had become so bitter and hostile that

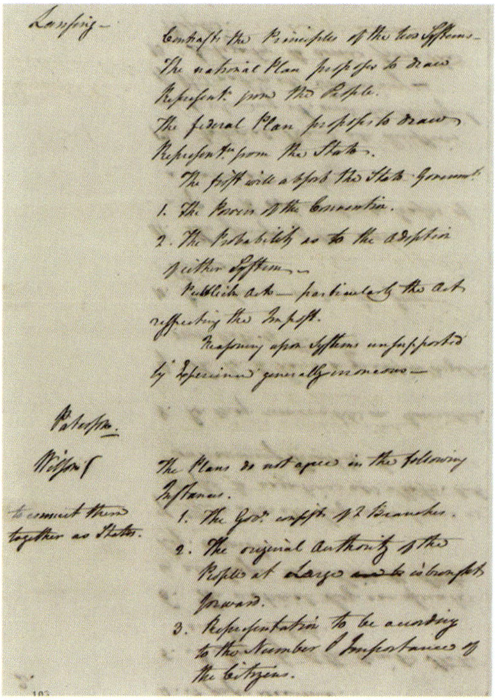

Shown here are William Paterson's notes from the Constitutional Convention.

Franklin, a man commonly known for his religious skepticism, suggested that a minister should open each session with a prayer to lessen the hostility. Upon hearing this, Hamilton is reported to have snapped that the convention could do its job without "the necessity of calling in foreign aid."[37]

At last, a stalemate was prevented when one of the committee members, Roger Sherman of Connecticut, rose to propose the creation of two houses of lawmakers. The number of representatives for a lower house—the House of Representatives—would be based on population. In the upper house, or the Senate, each state would have equal representation, regardless of the size of its population. Sherman's proposal drew fire from some who feared that it leaned too far in the direction of favoring states' rights over a functional federal government. Also, there still remained the unresolved issue of counting slaves.

Conflicting Views of Slavery

At the time, slavery prospered in the South and had almost vanished in the North. Some Northern delegates considered slavery to be immoral and something to be eliminated by law. Many Southerners, on the other hand, claimed that slaves were property, and protection of property was a fundamental duty of government. At the beginning of the convention, delegates had largely ignored this issue, fearing it would disrupt, if not ruin, the convention.

However, by June, slavery was a hot topic. In addition to arguing the moral aspects of slavery, some delegates also wondered how slaves would be considered in terms of taxes. Pierce Butler of South Carolina suggested that states that paid more in property taxes should have more power in Congress. To this, Massachusetts's Elbridge Gerry demanded to know how slaves should be counted. "Blacks are property," he said, "and are used to the southward as horses and cattle to the northward: and why should their representation be increased to the southward on account of the number of slaves, than horses or oxen to the north?"[38]

Gerry's sarcastic question underscored a larger issue: How should slaves be counted for purposes of representation? Delegates from states that relied heavily on slavery wanted slaves included in their population counts to boost their number of representatives, although they had no intention of letting slaves vote. Northern delegates, meanwhile, had no intention of letting southern states gain political power by means of what many considered an evil institution. The convention would not solve this problem until August.

A vote was finally called and resulted in a tie. Another committee, comprised of one member from each state, convened to break the impasse. At last, the group recommended a compromise: The House of Representatives would be based on population, with slaves counted as three-fifths of a person for purposes of taxes and representation only; in the Senate, states would all have exactly the same number of representatives. Such a system helped almost all the states. In the Senate, Northern states would enjoy greater representation in relation to their population, while the growing South with its slave-based economy would enjoy greater political strength in the House.

According to the compromise, voters would elect members of the House, who had to be at least 26 years old and serve two-year terms. State legislatures, however, would choose the country's senators, who had to be 30 years old and would serve six years at a time.

Members of the U.S. Senate were chosen by state legislatures until 1913. That year, the 17th Amendment to the U.S. Constitution allowed for the direct election of senators.

Final Compromises

At this point, there was little left for anyone to say. It was time to put the ideas into writing. On July 24, the delegates chose five men to act as a "Committee of Detail" to draft a constitution based on the agreements reached during the debates. On August 6, the convention met again. As delegates read their draft copies, controversy flared up once more. Suddenly, delegates from the South complained that if Congress, dominated by Northern states, had the power to regulate commerce, it could hurt the South's economy through export taxes. The slavery issue stirred once more, putting the convention in an uproar. Even Morris joined other critics from the North and denounced slavery as "the curse of heaven on the states where it prevailed."[39]

Angry Southerners responded that slavery was essential to their economy and way of life. The anger among the Southern faction was so strong that John Rutledge of South Carolina warned that the only question left was "whether the Southern states shall or shall not be parties to the Union."[40]

Finally, the convention produced another compromise. The antislavery faction agreed to a provision in the constitution that denied Congress the authority to regulate the slave trade before 1808. Any slaves imported during this time, however, would be subjected to an import tax. Northerners also agreed that slave owners could recover slaves who escaped to other states. In return, Southerners accepted constitutional language that made it easier for Northern states to

Shown here is the official seal of the President of the United States, the head of the nation's executive branch.

get certain navigation advantages they had long desired. Before the American Revolution, England had required that the colonists export their goods on British ships. Southerners, who had few merchant ships, had long worried that new laws could be passed that would require goods to be shipped on American vessels. Because the North owned most of the new nation's seagoing vessels, Southerners feared that Northern states could control the South's economy if lawmakers passed such a requirement. As such, Southern delegates wanted the constitution to require a two-thirds majority to make the passage of any navigation acts difficult. Now, though, because Southerners received concessions on the slave issue, they agreed that the two-thirds requirement be dropped.

The compromise also set forth provisions for the new government to coin money, regulate commerce, and make laws. A federal system was also set up that divided power among a lawmaking body, an executive branch led by a president that executes or carries out the laws, and a court system that enforces them. To assure that no branch would become too powerful, a system of checks and balances was officially created. For example, a president may veto, or cancel, a law passed by Congress. The lawmakers, however, can override his objection with a two-thirds majority.

Delegates worked out another compromise on electing a president. They crafted language that allowed only one executive—a person at least 35 years old and born in the United States—to serve for four years and be eligible to run for reelection. However, instead of voting directly for a president, voters would elect presidential electors to cast their votes for the best candidate.

In a concession to the advocates of states' rights, delegates agreed that Congress would not be able to declare state laws unconstitutional. In time, however, the federal judicial branch would assume this responsibility.

One sticking point remained: Many delegates complained that the plan they were developing had no bill of rights—a document that explicitly stated the rights of citizens. Though this omission troubled many delegates, the consensus was that such a bill was not needed at this point. Most state constitutions, some argued, already had such a bill. Moreover, others added, adding a bill of rights might seem like waving a red flag to citizens to signal there was something suspicious about the new constitution.

The Ratification Process

The delegates faced one more big question: Who should approve, or ratify, the new U.S. Constitution? One idea contained in the Virginia Plan was that after Congress had given its approval, an assembly composed of representatives from the states, elected by the people, should convene and vote. This idea was not popular, nor was calling for another national convention.

The Electoral College

In the United States, the president is not elected based on who wins the popular vote. Instead, as stated in the Constitution, the president is elected through a system called the Electoral College. The number of electors a state has is equal to how many senators and representatives the state has in Congress. As of 2016, the Electoral College has 538 members, and 270 electoral votes are needed for someone to be elected president.

Although it is not stated in the Constitution, it is common practice for electors to vote based on the popular vote in their state. However, because of the Electoral College system and the way votes are distributed through it, there have been multiple times in U.S. history when a presidential candidate lost the popular vote but won the presidency specifically because of the Electoral College: Rutherford B. Hayes in 1876, Benjamin Harrison in 1888, George W. Bush in 2000, and Donald Trump in 2016.

At the time the Constitution was written, the person who won the majority of the electoral votes became president and the runner-up became vice president. However, in 1804, the Constitution was changed so candidates run for either president or vice president and the electors vote for them separately. That is the only major change that has been made to this system since the Constitution was written.

Delegates also disliked letting the various state legislatures debate and vote on the document.

Finally, the delegates decided the Constitution was so important that it demanded popular ratification. This meant that once Congress ratified the document, states would set up special conventions where delegates would debate and vote on ratification. The convention further decided that ratification required approval of nine of the thirteen states, not a unanimous vote.

Closing the Convention

With delegates reaching the point of exhaustion, another special group—the Committee of Style and Arrangement—put the final touches on the Constitution. At last, the final document was ready on September 12. Among the most important alterations was the changing of the words in the preamble from "We, the people of the States of North Carolina, Virginia, Massachusetts, [and so forth]" to "We, the people of the United States." The new phrase was more than a change in style; it indicated that the Constitution

Franklin's Words of Praise

Like many of the delegates at the Constitutional Convention, Benjamin Franklin had doubts about certain parts of the Constitution. However, when the convention's work was done, he wrote a speech that praised his fellow delegates for their accomplishments and their willingness to compromise. After hearing Franklin's words, many delegates to state conventions overcame their reservations about the Constitution and signed it. Below is an excerpt from Franklin's speech:

> *I agree to this Constitution with all its faults—if they are such—because I think a general government necessary for us … I doubt, too whether any other convention we can obtain may be able to make a better Constitution; for, when you assemble a number of men, to have the advantage of their joint wisdom, you inevitably assemble with those men all their prejudices, their passions, their errors of opinion, their local interests, and their selfish views. From such an assembly can a perfect production be expected?*

> *It therefore astonishes me … to find this system approaching as near to perfection as it does; and I think it will astonish our enemies, who are waiting with confidence to hear that our councils are confounded … and that our States are on the point of separation, only to meet hereafter for the purpose of cutting one another's throats.*[1]

1. Quoted in Walter Isaacson, *Benjamin Franklin: An American Life*. New York, NY: Simon & Schuster, 2003, pp. 457–458.

Benjamin Franklin

was a framework for a government that bound together the American people as a whole and not as a loose group of citizens from individual states. It solidified the sense of a unified American identity, which was not felt under the Articles of Confederation.

Before the delegates could go home, Franklin asked them to join him in signing the historic document. He, like most—if not all—the delegates, had reservations about what they had done. However, he was still amazed that they had done so well. A perfect document, he told his colleagues, would never be possible, given the diversity of opinion in the convention. "Thus," he said, "I consent, Sir, to this Constitution because I expect no better and because I am not sure that it is not the best."[41]

Morris also had objections, but he signed anyway. "The moment this plan goes forth," he predicted, "all other considerations will be laid aside and the great question will be, shall there be a national government or not? This must take place, or a general anarchy will be the alternative."[42]

Three delegates had such strong misgivings over the document, however, that they could not sign. Randolph, who had introduced the Virginia Plan, now said, "In refusing to sign the Constitution, I take a step which may be the most awful of my life, but it is not possible for me to hesitate, much less change."[43] Gerry and Mason also refused to sign.

All others, except those who had left the convention, signed their names to the document they had struggled to create. After the signing, the convention adjourned. Delegates dined at a local tavern, made their farewells, and prepared for their long journeys home. Their work was done, but the story of the Constitution was far from over.

Chapter Six

DEBATING THE DOCUMENT

The Constitutional Convention did not have the final say on whether or not the Constitution would formally go into effect as the backbone of the U.S. government. That was left up to the states. As the delegates returned home from Philadelphia, they could only wait to see if the states approved the document they had worked so hard on and compromised so successfully to create.

As state ratification conferences began, the delegates to those official meetings were not the only Americans spending their time debating the document. The new U.S. Constitution was something that mattered to all Americans, and, as such, citizens learned about the document through pamphlets and newspapers before discussing it with one another. Lively debates sprang up in homes, taverns, and other public places, and it soon became clear that the nation was divided over the document—with each side feeling passionately about its position.

The American people generally fell into one of two camps concerning the ratification of the Constitution. Federalists supported ratification, while Anti-Federalists did not. This divide was present among Americans from all walks of life, including writers and political leaders, who used their voices to argue their positions to the public.

Anti-Federalist essays were published in newspapers around the country. The men who wrote these essays did so under pen names that included Centinel and Cato. In response to the attacks against the Constitution, Hamilton, Madison, and Jay published a series of 85 essays defending the document they helped create. These essays are known today as the Federalist Papers, and they continue to serve as a guide to the ideas behind the Constitution and the mindsets of those who believed in this document and the government it established.

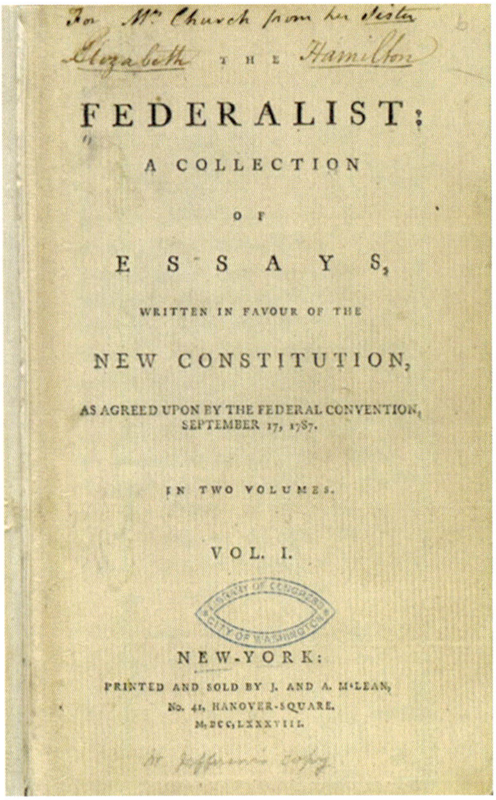

The essays that make up the Federalist Papers were all written under the pen name Publius. However, today we know that the majority of those essays were written by Hamilton, who was the sole author of 51 of the 85.

A Divided Nation

Federalists enjoyed a few advantages in the debate. For one thing, the Constitution represented the work of a group of respected national leaders, such as Washington and Franklin. Federalists also offered many Americans something to rally behind: a specific plan to save the union from falling apart.

In contrast, as Madison noted of the Massachusetts Anti-Federalists, "There was not a single character capable of uniting their wills or directing their measures ... They had no plan whatever."[44] Instead, historian Catherine Drinker Bowen stated, "Anti-federalists worked on the people's fear; they viewed with alarm, harped on the novelty, the experimental nature of the program."[45] Some of these critics proclaimed that delegates had created the Constitution in secrecy and produced a document that was intended to benefit only the wealthy and the privileged. A Massachusetts Anti-Federalist complained, "These lawyers, and men of learning and moneyed men, that ... make us poor illiterate people swallow down the pill ... they will swallow up all us little folks ... just as the whale swallowed up Jonah!"[46]

Critics also warned that a strong federal government would take away their liberties. Some suggested that if a capital city, such as Washington, D.C., was established as called for in the Constitution, Americans could expect it to become a dangerous, armed camp. Setting up a vice presidency was also considered dangerous because it could create a rival to the president. Various church leaders complained that framers did not make Christianity part of the Constitution. One Protestant Christian, however, "shuddered at the idea that Roman Catholics, papists and pagans might be introduced into office and that popery [the Catholic leadership] and the Inquisition [torture once used by the Catholic Church] may be established in America."[47]

Anti-Federalists successfully created a strong resistance to the Constitution by playing on Americans' fears and uncertainties, but their cause was weakened because they were divided in their opposition. Northern critics, for example, complained that the Constitution did not end slavery, while southern planters argued it did not fully protect the institution.

Economic and social factors often determined which side of the argument Americans chose. Many bankers, factory owners, professionals, wealthy landowners, and officers in the American Revolution filled the ranks of Federalists. Anti-Federalists, meanwhile, tended to be tradesmen, farmers, and those who supported economic policies that favored debtors. In addition, some state government officials also opposed ratification because they feared losing power and control to a central government. As historian Richard B. Morris explained, "The anti federalists often looked very much like a group of state and local officeholders concerned about their vested interests."[48]

The anti-ratification movement was inspired in some ways by the revolutionary movement that led Americans to break away from Britain. Memories of British oppression were still fresh for many, and they feared a strong national government would cause similar problems. Older Americans who remembered the abuses of the oppressive British government were more likely than younger people to oppose a stronger central government. Ironically, many Americans who were once considered radicals during the period leading up to the American Revolution now looked at the younger generation of Federalists as the new radicals.

Geography also played a role in dividing America into two camps. According to author William Peters,

> *Federalist power was located mostly in the settled, eastern sections of the states. Anti-federalism was generally strongest in the back-country and frontier areas, regions that had been underrepresented in the Convention. Far from the centers of political power in their own states, backcountry Americans saw themselves as certain to be even more remote from the seat of some new national government.*[49]

Although the American public was bitterly divided over the issue of ratification, they were not the deciding factor in whether or not the document was approved. That was left up to the men chosen to represent their interests at state ratification conventions. Like the men who created the Constitution, everyday Americans could do little except wait to see what came out of those conventions.

Ratification Becomes a Reality

The debate in the American public mirrored the clashes taking place during the state ratification conventions. On September 28, 1787, Pennsylvania's Federalists were so eager to ratify that they tried to push a proposal through the

Defending the Document

The following paragraphs are part of a letter written by a special committee and approved by the members of the Constitutional Convention that explains why the delegates decided to draft a plan for a new government instead of revising the old one:

It is obviously impracticable in the federal government of these states to secure all rights of independent sovereignty [independent power] to each, and yet provide for the interest and safety of all. Individuals entering into society must give up a share of liberty to preserve the rest. The magnitude of the sacrifice must depend as well on situation and circumstance as on the object to be obtained. It is at all times difficult to draw … the line between those rights which must be surrendered and those which may be reserved; and on the present occasion, this difficulty was increased by a difference among the several states as to their situation, extent, habits and particular interests.

In all our deliberations on this subject we kept steadily in our view that which appears to us the greatest interest of every true American: the consolidation of our union … thus the Constitution which we now present is the result of a spirit of … [friendship and compromise].

That it will meet the full and entire approbation [approval] of every state is not perhaps to be expected; but … that it may promote the lasting welfare of the country so dear to us all, and secure her freedom and happiness, is our most ardent [passionate] wish.[1]

1. Quoted in William Peters, *A More Perfect Union: The Making of the United States Constitution*. New York, NY: Crown, 1987, p. 216.

state assembly authorizing a ratification convention, even though official notification concerning the Constitution had not yet arrived. When 19 Anti-Federalists boycotted the session to prevent having the required minimum number of lawmakers, an angry mob forcibly abducted two of them from a nearby boardinghouse and dragged them kicking and fighting into the session. The assembly then had the minimum number of required participants and established the first Tuesday in November as the day to vote for convention delegates.

At last, the Pennsylvania ratification convention got underway on November 21, 1787. Though outnumbered, Anti-Federalists rose to state their cases against ratification. Some complained that the Constitutional Convention exceeded its authority. Others were upset that the Constitution had no bill of rights.

Any hopes among Federalists that Pennsylvania would be the first state to ratify the Constitution were dashed when news came that Delaware had unanimously approved the Constitution on December 7 after just five days of debate. Under the final draft of the Constitution, smaller states such as Delaware stood to gain power and influence that exceeded their population or wealth. This made the ratification process easy for Delaware because its leaders supported the document. Debate in Pennsylvania raged on for weeks, but delegates finally ratified the Constitution on December 12.

By January 9, 1788, Georgia, Connecticut, and New Jersey had also voted for ratification. A month of contentious debate in Boston, Massachusetts, ended in favor of the Federalists when distinguished Anti-Federalists Samuel Adams and John Hancock changed their minds and joined the Federalists. The state assembly ratified the Constitution but recommended that it be amended in the future. During the spring, Maryland also voted for ratification by a vote of 63 to 11. A small number of Anti-Federalists, however, signed a letter of protest: "We consider the proposed form of government very defective, and that the liberty and happiness of the people will be endangered if the system be not greatly changed and altered."[50] This was a common theme in many states: Although the document was ratified, many still spoke out against it or called for extensive changes to be made to it in the immediate future. Chief among those proposed changes was the inclusion of a bill of rights.

Almost a month after Maryland's vote, South Carolina also ratified the Constitution. Though the slavery issue

The first page of the U.S. Constitution is shown here. The document officially went into effect on June 21, 1788, and has continued to serve as the framework of American democracy ever since that date.

Celebrating with Songs

Like many other places in America, Boston erupted into celebration after its state convention ratified the Constitution. In addition to the cheers, toasts, and ringing of church bells, Bostonians sang this song to the tune of "Yankee Doodle":

The 'Vention did in Boston meet,
The State House could not hold 'em,
So then they went to Fed'ral Steet,
And there the truth was told 'em …
And ev'ry morning went to prayer,
And then began disputing,
Till oppositions silenced were,
By arguments refuting.
Then 'Squire Hancock like a man,
Who dearly loved the nation,
By a conciliatory plan,
Prevented much vexation.
He made a woundy Fed'ral speech,
With sense and elocution;
And then the 'Vention did beseech
T' adopt the Constitution.
Now politicians of all kinds,
Who are not yet decided,
May see how Yankees speak their minds, And yet are not divided.
So here I end my Fed'ral song, Composed of thirteen verses;
May agriculture flourish long
And commerce fill our purses![1]

1. Quoted in Catherine Drinker Bowen, *Miracle at Philadelphia: The Story of the Constitutional Convention, May to September 1787*. Boston, MA: Little, Brown and Company, 1966, pp. 291–292.

bitterly divided delegates in New Hampshire, they eventually voted to ratify on June 21, 1788, with a vote of 57 to 47, becoming the necessary ninth state to make the Constitution legal. A new union had officially formed.

The Final States

Two of the nation's most important states, though, had not yet voted. Virginia was essential to the nation because of its size, and New York was a prominent state (with New York City being an especially prominent city) because of its important location on the Atlantic. Many Americans could not conceive of how the nation could function without them. For the moment, however, these states were still locked in controversy.

In Virginia, where Anti-Federalists were in the majority, Colonel William Grayson mocked the Federalist claim that a strong central government was needed to ward off national threats:

> *Pennsylvania and Maryland are to fall upon us from the north like the Goths and Vandals of old ... the Indians are to invade us from our rears ... And the Carolinians from the South, mounted on alligators, I presume, are to come and destroy our cornfields and eat up our little children. These Sir, are the mighty dangers which await us if we reject the Constitution.*[51]

In a more serious tone, Patrick Henry warned, "The American spirit, assisted by the ropes and chains of consolidation [federalism] is about to convert this country into a powerful and mighty empire ... There be no checks, no real balances in this government."[52]

Despite such colorful language, Anti-Federalists were losing the battle in Virginia. On the first day of debate, Edmund Randolph shocked and angered his Anti-Federalist allies by defecting to the other side. He explained that he had taken this action to preserve the nation. The union "is the anchor of our political salvation; and I will assent to the lopping off of this limb," he said, pointing to his arm, "before I assent to the dissolution of the union."[53] A wave of anger from the Anti-Federalists could not stop a majority of the delegation from ratifying the Constitution on June 25. However, the delegates also called for amendments when the new Congress assembled for the first time.

Many Anti-Federalists in Virginia, however, found defeat hard to take. At a protest meeting in Richmond, they discussed ways to prevent the Constitution from working, but Patrick Henry advised them to drop the matter. Then, he urged his fellow Anti-Federalists "as true and faithful republicans [members of a republic] you had all better go home."[54] They were fighting a losing battle, and the preservation of the young nation was seen by many as more important than their issues with the new government. The Constitution was not perfect, but it would keep the country together.

News that Virginia had ratified the Constitution rattled the Anti-Federalists in New York, but they refused to surrender. One Anti-Federalist proposed that New York should be able to quit the new union if its suggestions for amendments were not adopted. In response, Hamilton suggested that New York City and the state's southern counties should join the union without the rest of New York. Neither motion, however, won approval. On July 26, New York also voted for ratification. Delegates recommended a bill of rights and 32 other amendments.

As other states celebrated ratification with parades and marches, North Carolina and Rhode Island remained undecided. North Carolina did not immediately follow its neighbor Virginia's example, as many had expected. Instead, its ratification convention voted to do nothing until another national convention was held to discuss amending the Constitution.

George Washington was the natural choice to serve as the first president of the United States. He shaped the executive branch of the U.S. government through the choices he made while serving in this role.

The other states, however, showed little interest in another convention. Instead, Peters wrote, "In place of a new convention, North Carolinians were soon confronted by a new government, leaving them in the uncomfortable status of foreigners."[55] The other states, in fact, moved forward without North Carolina and Rhode Island. On February 4, 1789, electors chose George Washington as the nation's first president and John Adams as vice president. A new national government began to function—one based on the principles of the U.S. Constitution.

The Bill of Rights

When the first U.S. Congress met in March 1789 in New York City, it took up the matter of amendments to the Constitution. Madison, now a member of the Virginia delegation to the U.S. House of Representatives, kept a pledge he had made at the Virginia state ratification conference to create a bill of rights. Not trusting what could happen in another national convention, Madison instead urged Congress to use the amendment process outlined in Article V of the Constitution. According to this article, Congress must approve an amendment by a two-thirds majority before the president signs it. Next, three-fourths of the state governments must ratify the proposed amendment within a set timeframe.

Out of the hundreds of amendments proposed in Congress, only 12 survived.

From this dozen, the states ratified 10 by December 15, 1791. Known collectively as the Bill of Rights, these amendments guarantee the well-known rights to freedom of religion, freedom of the press, freedom of speech, freedom to peacefully assemble, and freedom to petition government to address grievances. Under the Bill of Rights, Americans also have the right to carry weapons and to be safe from "unreasonable searches and seizures" by law enforcement. People officially charged with a crime do not have to testify against themselves thanks to these amendments.

Congress of the United States

The Bill of Rights is one of the most famous parts of the U.S. Constitution.

According to these first 10 amendments, those charged with a crime are also entitled to "due process of law," or legal procedural safeguards. In addition, they have a right to a speedy trial and a trial by jury. The accused must be informed of the specific charges brought against them, be able to confront all witnesses testifying against them, and have access to an attorney. Americans are also protected from excessive bail and cruel and unusual punishment. In addition, the Bill of Rights clearly outlines that any powers not specifically reserved for the federal government in the Constitution belong to the states or the people. This was an important point to include because of the value placed on protecting states' rights during both the Constitutional Convention and the state ratification conventions.

By the time these rights became part of the Constitution, North Carolina and Rhode Island had also ratified the document. At last, all the former colonies were united under a new national government—the country's second in less than two decades. The new document at the center of this government, however, would prove to be far more enduring than the one that came before it. It has lasted for more than two centuries.

Epilogue

CHALLENGES AND CHANGES

The U.S. Constitution was built to last. The men who met in Philadelphia in 1787 to create a better government for the United States drafted a document that has been able to withstand the challenges and changes that come with the passage of time. The Constitution is structured with enough detail to provide a solid foundation for the U.S. government, but it is also flexible enough to allow for changes as the nation evolves beyond anything the Founding Fathers imagined.

Debates about the Constitution are still a part of American life. They take place in classrooms, in courthouses, around kitchen tables, and on news programs. During these debates, many participants wonder what the men who wrote the Constitution would think of how the document is applied in America today. That is a difficult question to answer, though; America is certainly not the same as it was when those men first drafted the document. For example, the phrase "We the People" that opens the Constitution now applies to many more Americans than it did at the time that phrase was written. As Stephen Breyer, a current associate justice of the U.S. Supreme Court, has written, "As history has made clear, the original Constitution was insufficient. It did not include a majority of the nation within its 'democratic community.'"[56] Today, a much larger number of Americans—including women, African Americans, and Native Americans—are part of this "democratic community," thanks to important changes to the Constitution.

Major Amendments

For more than two centuries, the American people have expanded constitutional protection through the amendment process. Some of these changes came about as a result of the American Civil War.

Hip-Hop and History

In 2015, the story of the creation of the U.S. government made its way to Broadway. *Hamilton: An American Musical*, which depicts the life of Alexander Hamilton from the American Revolution through his death following a duel with vice president Aaron Burr, gained instant fame for its use of hip-hop and its multiracial casting of the Founding Fathers and other roles. The diversity of the musical's cast highlights creator Lin-Manuel Miranda's goal of telling America's creation story with people who were not originally included in that story because of their race or gender. As Leslie Odom Jr., who played Aaron Burr in the original Broadway cast of the musical, said, "It is quite literally taking the history that someone has tried to exclude us from and reclaiming it … We are saying we have the right to tell it too."[1]

Hamilton quickly became a huge success, selling out shows months in advance. It won 11 Tony Awards for excellence in Broadway theater. Its popularity has proven that American history can be fun and entertaining for people of all ages and backgrounds if presented in a fresh way. It has allowed a new generation of Americans to understand this chapter in the history of the United States by relating it to a world they understand and appreciate, helping more Americans feel connected to their nation's roots.

1. Quoted in Mark Binelli, "*Hamilton* Creator Lin-Manuel Miranda: The Rolling Stone Interview," *Rolling Stone*, June 1, 2016. www.rollingstone.com/music/features/hamilton-creator-lin-manuel-miranda-the-rolling-stone-interview-20160601.

Hamilton: An American Musical *tells the story of America's early years as an independent nation in a modern, relatable way.*

Women took to the streets in the early 1900s to call for an amendment granting them the right to vote.

Within a few years after the conclusion of the war in 1865, the nation ratified a trio of amendments meant to include freed male slaves and all black men in the democratic process. The 13th Amendment outlawed slavery, the 14th Amendment provided citizenship and due process of the law to former slaves, and the 15th Amendment forbade the use of race as a means of denying the right to vote. Almost 100 years later, during the height of the civil rights movement of the 1960s, the nation approved the 24th Amendment in 1964 to outlaw the use of poll taxes—taxes a voter must pay—that were still being used in many southern states to keep black Americans from voting.

Democracy took another step forward with the 19th Amendment, which was ratified in 1920. This amendment gave American women suffrage, or the right to vote. Suffrage was expanded to younger Americans in 1971, with ratification of the 26th Amendment that lowered the voting age from 21 to 18.

Not all efforts to expand equality through the amendment process, however, have been successful. Many Americans were disappointed when the country failed in the 1970s to ratify what at that time would have been the 27th Amendment, which they called the Equal Rights Amendment (ERA). Its supporters believed this amendment was necessary to protect females from unfair discrimination and to grant equal rights to all women in America. Though polls showed overwhelming support for the measure among the American public, only 35 out of the necessary 38 states had ratified the amendment by the 1979 deadline. It ultimately was not passed, but some groups are still working toward the ratification of this amendment today.

Interpreting the Constitution

In addition to the amendment process, the nation has also relied on judicial review to apply the Constitution's ideals to modern times. Judicial review is a procedure by which the U.S. Supreme Court decides whether certain laws or government practices violate the Constitution. Making this determination, however, is often difficult and can even seem arbitrary. Sometimes the Supreme Court has ruled in contradictory ways about the constitutionality of laws. In 1896 for instance, the Supreme Court upheld a Louisiana law that segregated railroad passengers based on their race in the case of *Plessy v. Ferguson*. The Court was persuaded that segregation that allowed "separate but equal" facilities was constitutional under the 14th Amendment. However, in 1954 in *Brown v. Board of Education of Topeka*, a unanimous Supreme Court reversed itself, now saying that, in the field of education, segregation violated the 14th Amendment, because separate educational facilities were inherently unequal. As former chief justice Charles

The U.S. Supreme Court's ruling in the case of Brown v. Board of Education of Topeka *proved that the idea of what is and is not interpreted to be constitutional can change over time. This flexibility has allowed America to evolve instead of remaining stuck in the same place it was in 1787.*

Evans Hughes once observed, "The Constitution is what the judges say it is."[57]

Judicial interpretations are often controversial. Millions of Americans, for example, were shocked in 1857 when the U.S. Supreme Court used the Constitution to determine that Dred Scott, a runaway slave, could not sue for his freedom because he was another man's property and had "no rights which any white man was bound to respect."[58] Although the Court ruled at that time that a black human being had no expectation of constitutional protections, it later decided that big businesses did deserve such protection. Some scholars state that the Supreme Court's ruling in *Santa Clara County v. Southern Pacific Railroad Co.* paved the way for the idea of "corporate personhood"—the idea that a business corporation is entitled to constitutional protection as if it were a person.

Over the years, the Supreme Court has often had to rule on many issues—including pornography, the medical use of marijuana, government spying on the Internet, and same-sex marriage—that the Founding Fathers never envisioned. Thus, justices often must interpret the "spirit" or "intent" of the Constitution as new issues emerge. They try to do this by studying previous cases, speeches made by lawmakers, and commentaries such as the Federalist Papers to find clues to what the original intent or principle may be. Often the task is difficult if not impossible. As Breyer has noted, "The First Amendment's language says the Congress shall not abridge 'the freedom of speech.' But it does not define 'the freedom of speech' in any detail."[59]

Critics, meanwhile, who think justices interpret the Constitution too freely, accuse them of being activist judges and interpreting the Constitution to comply with their personal beliefs. Others, however, worry that justices who use too much "judicial restraint" may render decisions that are unjust to citizens in an ever-changing world.

A clue to what the framers may have thought of this dilemma comes from Edmund Randolph, who was a member of the Committee of Detail in Philadelphia and helped write the finished draft of the Constitution. Instead of using specific words, he explained, the committee strove "to insert essential principles only," to keep the government from becoming "clogged" so that the Constitution could change with "times and events." Randolph added that the committee also tried "to use simple and precise language and general propositions."[60] Taking Randolph's words into account, the Constitution can truly be viewed as a living document that was specifically designed to change as America itself changed.

The Story Continues

The U.S. government has faced many challenges since the creation of the Constitution, but that document continues to provide the solid foundation for a strong democracy that protects the liberties of its citizens. When the Founding Fathers met in Philadelphia to revise the Articles of Confederation, they did not know they

Constitutional rights, such as the right to peacefully assemble, are just as important today as they were in the early years of the United States.

would emerge with plans for a new government, and they certainly did not know that this government would become known as the standard for democracy around the world. However, that is exactly what they created. The document they drafted and the amendments that have been made to it over the last two centuries are a testament to the importance of discussion, compromise, and forward thinking. The vision of the Founding Fathers and the hard work of those who have interpreted the Constitution from the 18th century through modern times have allowed this document to remain relevant longer than any other national constitution in use today.

The Constitution continues to provide U.S. leaders with guidance and continues to guard the individual liberties the Founding Fathers fought so hard to secure. The American story is a story of individuals coming together to form—in the words of the Constitution—"a more perfect Union," and it is up to each generation of Americans to make sure that story continues.

Notes

Chapter One: Creating an American Identity

1. J. Hector St. John de Crèvecoeur, *Letters from an American Farmer*. New York, NY: Fox, Duffield & Company, 1904, p. 55.
2. Quoted in William Miller, *A New History of the United States*. New York, NY: George Braziller, 1958, p. 46.
3. Quoted in William Bennett, *America: The Last Best Hope, vol. 1, From the Age of Discovery to a World at War, 1492–1914*. Nashville, TN: Nelson Current, 2006, p. 40.
4. Richard B. Morris and Editors of *Life, The New World: Prehistory to 1774*. New York, NY: *Time*, 1963, p. 119.
5. Paul Johnson, *A History of the American People*. New York, NY: HarperCollins, 1997, p. 116.
6. Daniel J. Boorstin, *The Americans: The Colonial Experience*. New York, NY: Random House, 1958, p. 151.
7. David McCullough, *1776*. New York, NY: Simon & Schuster, 2005, p. 23.
8. Quoted in Johnson, *A History of the American People*, p. 137.
9. Quoted in Johnson, *A History of the American People*, p. 137.

Chapter Two: Opposing Tyranny

10. Quoted in Walter Isaacson, *Benjamin Franklin: An American Life*. New York, NY: Simon & Schuster, 2003, pp. 161–162.
11. Francis D. Cogliano, "Was the American Revolution Inevitable?" BBC, February 17, 2011. www.bbc.co.uk/history/british/empire_seapower/american_revolution_01.shtml.
12. Thomas Fleming, "Fleming: What Life Was Like in 1776," *Wall Street Journal*, July 2, 2012. www.wsj.com/articles/SB10001424052702303561504577496620544901322.
13. Howard Zinn, *A People's History of the United States*. New York, NY: Harper & Row, 1980, p. 65.
14. Quoted in Zinn, *A People's History of the United States*, p. 65.
15. Samuel Eliot Morison, *The Oxford*

History of the American People: Prehistory to 1789*. New York, NY: Penguin, 1991, p. 245.

16. Morison, *The Oxford History of the American People: Prehistory to 1789*, p. 246.

Chapter Three: Fighting for Liberty

17. Quoted in McCullough, *1776*, p. 49.
18. Quoted in Isaacson, *Benjamin Franklin: An American Life*, p. 296.
19. Quoted in Sculley Bradley, ed., *The American Tradition in Literature*. New York, NY: Norton & Company, 1967, p. 290.
20. Quoted in George Seldes, *The Great Thoughts*. New York, NY: Ballantine, 1985, p. 319.
21. Quoted in Bennett, *From the Age of Discovery to a World at War, 1492–1914*, p. 82.
22. Quoted in Stephen Ambrose and Douglas Brinkley, *Witness to America: An Illustrated Documentary History of the United States from the Revolution to Today*. New York, NY: HarperCollins, 1999, p. 17.
23. Quoted in Bennett, *From the Age of Discovery to a World at War, 1492–1914*, p. 86.
24. Quoted in Bennett, *From the Age of Discovery to a World at War, 1492–1914*, p. 86.
25. Quoted in William Miller, *A New History of The United States*. New York, NY: George Braziller, Inc., 1958, p. 94.

Chapter Four: Governing the New Nation

26. Quoted in Zinn, *A People's History of the United States*, p. 88.
27. Quoted in Richard B. Morris and Editors of *Life, The Making of a Nation: 1775–1789*. New York, NY: *Time*, 1963, p. 104.
28. Quoted in Morris and Editors of *Life, The Making of a Nation: 1775–1789*, p. 112.
29. Quoted in Richard Haesly, ed., *The Constitutional Convention*. San Diego, CA: Greenhaven, 2002, p. 45.
30. Quoted in Isaacson, *Benjamin Franklin: An American Life*, p. 445.

Chapter Five: The Constitutional Convention

31. Charles L. Mee Jr., *The Genius of the People*. New York, NY: Harper & Row, 1987, pp. 60–61.
32. Quoted in William Peters, *A More Perfect Union: The Making of the U.S. Constitution*. New York, NY: Crown, 1987, p. 23.
33. Quoted in Morris and Editors of *Life, The Making of a Nation*, p. 131.
34. William K. Stevens, "Behind the Scenes in 1787: Secrecy in the Heat," *New York Times*, May 25, 1987. www.nytimes.com/1987/05/25/us/behind-the-scenes-in-1787-secrecy-in-the-heat.html.
35. Quoted in Isaacson, *Benjamin Franklin: An American Life*, p. 451.
36. Quoted in Catherine Drinker Bowen, *Miracle at Philadelphia: The Story of the Constitutional Convention, May to September 1787*. Boston, MA: Little, Brown and Company, 1966, p. 131.
37. Quoted in Morris and Editors of *Life, The New World: Prehistory to 1774*, p. 131.
38. Quoted in The Avalon Project, "Notes of the Secret Debates of the Federal Convention of 1787, Taken by the Late Hon Robert Yates, Chief Justice of the State of New York, and One of the Delegates from That State to the Said Convention," Yale Law School, 2008. avalon.law.yale.edu/18th_century/yates.asp.
39. Quoted in Mee, *The Genius of the People*, p. 248.
40. Quoted in Mee, *The Genius of the People*, p. 221.
41. Quoted in Peters, *A More Perfect Union: The Making of the U.S. Constitution*, p. 211.
42. Quoted in Peters, *A More Perfect Union: The Making of the U.S. Constitution*, p. 213.
43. Quoted in Peters, *A More Perfect Union: The Making of the U.S. Constitution*, p. 214.

Chapter Six: Debating the Document

44. Quoted in Roger A. Bruns, *A More Perfect Union: The Creation of the U.S. Constitution: An Introduction*. Washington, DC: National Archives Trust Fund Board, 1986, p. 8.
45. Bowen, *Miracle at Philadelphia*, pp. 271–327.
46. Quoted in Bruns, *A More Perfect Union: The Creation of the U.S.

Constitution: An Introduction*, p. 10.

47. Quoted in Bowen, *Miracle at Philadelphia*, pp. 285–286.
48. Morris and Editors of *Life*, *The New World: Prehistory to 1774*, p. 134.
49. Peters, *A More Perfect Union: The Making of the U.S. Constitution*, p. 226.
50. Quoted in Bowen, *Miracle at Philadelphia*, p. 293.
51. Quoted in Bowen, *Miracle at Philadelphia*, p. 298.
52. Quoted in Bowen, *Miracle at Philadelphia*, pp. 297–298.
53. Quoted in Peters, *A More Perfect Union: The Making of the U.S. Constitution*, p. 231.
54. Quoted in Bowen, *Miracle at Philadelphia*, pp. 304–305.
55. Peters, *A More Perfect Union: The Making of the U.S. Constitution*, p. 234.

Epilogue: Challenges and Changes

56. Stephen Breyer, *Active Liberty: Interpreting Our Democratic Constitution*. New York, NY: Alfred A. Knopf, 2005, p. 32.
57. Quoted in "Charles Evans Hughes," Columbia250, 2004. c250.columbia.edu/c250_celebrates/remarkable_columbians/charles_hughes.html.
58. Quoted in John M. Blum, William S. McFeely, Edmund S. Morgan, Arthur M. Schlesinger Jr., Kenneth M. Stampp, and C. Vann Woodward, *The National Experience: A History of the United States*, 6th ed. San Diego, CA: Harcourt Brace Jovanovich, 1985, p. 336.
59. Breyer, *Active Liberty*, p. 45.
60. Quoted in Peters, *A More Perfect Union: The Making of the U.S. Constitution*, p. 135.

For More Information

Books

Hamilton, Alexander, John Jay, and James Madison. *The Federalist Papers*. London, UK: Arcturus Publishing Limited, 2016.
The latest edition of *The Federalist Papers* continues to provide unique insight into the U.S. Constitution through the words of three of its fiercest defenders.

Hennessey, Jonathan, and Aaron McConnell. *The United States Constitution: A Graphic Adaptation*. New York, NY: Hill and Wang, 2008.
Hennessey and McConnell present the articles and amendments that make up the Constitution as we know it today using the engaging format of a graphic novel.

Klarman, Michael J. *The Framers' Coup: The Making of the United States Constitution*. New York, NY: Oxford University Press, 2016.
This comprehensive volume details the difficult process that led to the creation of the Constitution, often using direct quotes from those who were there.

Madison, James. *Writings*. New York, NY: Library of America, 1999.
This collection of Madison's writings—from his time as a framer of the Constitution through his presidency and retirement—features notes by historian Jack N. Rakove.

Miranda, Lin-Manuel, and Jeremy McCarter. *Hamilton: The Revolution*. New York, NY: Grand Central Publishing, 2016.
Readers enter the world of the groundbreaking historical musical *Hamilton* as they discover the complete lyrics to the musical's songs and the stories behind both the musical itself and the Founding Fathers who inspired it.

Nelson, Kristen Rajczak. *U.S. Constitution*. New York, NY: PowerKids Press, 2016.
This book features a variety of relevant primary sources, as well as a comprehensive breakdown of the many articles of the Constitution using language young people will easily understand.

Travis, Cathy. *Constitution Translated for Kids*. Austin, TX: Synergy Books, 2006.
This volume uses simple, accessible language and additional historical context to help young people understand the text of the Constitution.

Websites

The Constitution of the United States (www.archives.gov/founding-docs/constitution)
The National Archives provides a closer look at the Constitution through relevant articles, answers to common questions, and images of the document.

Hamilton's America: A Documentary Film (www.pbs.org/wnet/gperf/episodes/hamiltons-america/)
The official website of PBS's documentary about the musical *Hamilton* presents historical facts and behind-the-scenes content to introduce a new audience—especially young people—to an essential chapter in American history.

National Constitution Center (constitutioncenter.org)
The National Constitution Center is an institution created to promote a nonpartisan understanding of the Constitution through education and debate.

Primary Documents in American History: United States Constitution (www.loc.gov/rr/program/bib/ourdocs/Constitution.html)
The Library of Congress has links to many relevant primary sources that can be used to enhance an understanding of the Constitution.

1600 Penn (www.whitehouse.gov/1600)
The official White House website invites people to learn more about the U.S. government through links to pages about each branch, as well as the Constitution itself.

Index

A

Adams, John
- chosen vice president, 84
- Constitutional Convention and, 64
- First Continental Congress and, 35
- on Jefferson writing Declaration of Independence, 42
- on Washington chosen to lead Continental Army, 39
- on writings of Paine, 42

Adams, Samuel, 30, 81

African Americans
- in American Revolution, 54
- judicial review and, 89
- as part of democratic community, 86
- voting rights, 9, 54
- *See also* slaves/slavery

Albany Plan of Union, 27

Allen, Ethan, 37

American identity
- American Revolution and, 37, 51
- colonial era development of, 12, 18, 22, 25–26
- Constitution and, 8, 63, 76

American Revolution
- African Americans in, 54
- battles, 7–8, 36, 46–49, 54
- beginning of, 7–8, 36
- British sympathizers, 45, 49
- Continental army, 39, 43–44, 53
- creation of American identity and, 37, 51
- debts from, 51, 56, 58
- destruction from, 51
- Enlightenment and, 24–25, 42, 65
- treaty, 7, 49–50, 58
- Washington chosen as Army leader, 38–39
- wounded soldiers, 44
- *See also* taxes, colonial era

Anglican Church. *See* Church of England

Anti-Federalists
- characteristics of, 78–79
- public arguments of, 77
- in state conventions, 80–81, 83–84

Arnold, Benedict, 37, 40, 46

Articles of Confederation
- national government under, 8, 55, 60, 63
- state governments under, 51, 56–57

B

Baltimore, Lord, 16

Bedford, Gunning, 69

Bill of Rights (U.S.)
- added to Constitution, 7, 81, 84–85
- First Amendment, 85
- not in Constitution, 73

Boorstin, David, 24

Boston (Massachusetts),
- British evacuated, 40
- violence in, 30–33

Boston Massacre, 32–33

Boston Tea Party, 33–34

Bowen, Catherine Drinker, 78

bread colonies, 19

Breyer, Stephen, 86, 90

British Bill of Rights (1689), 20

Brown University, 24

Brown v. Board of Education of Topeka, 89

Burgoyne, John, 46

Burnaby, Andrew, 17

Bush, George W., 74

businesses, 52, 90

Butler, Pierce, 70

C

Canada
- borders extended, 35
- Continental army in, 40
- Hudson River and, 46
- loyalists in, 52
- under British rule, 27

Catholics, 14–16, 23, 78

Cato, 77

Centinel, 77

Charleston (South Carolina), 16, 35, 40, 48

Church of England, 15, 23–24, 53

cities, growth of, 16, 18

Civil War Amendments, 9, 86, 88

Clinton, Henry, 48

Cochran, John, 44

Cogliano, Francis D., 28

colonists
- development of American identity and, 12, 18, 22, 25–26
- economic reasons for founding, 14
- Native Americans and, 13–14, 21
- non-English, 13, 16
- regional differences, 18–19
- religious reasons for founding, 15–16
- reluctance to declare independence from England, 37

rights as Englishmen, 20
troops for French and Indian War, 26–27
See also government, in colonies; taxes, colonial era
Columbia University, 24
Columbus, Christopher, 13–14
Committee of Detail, 71, 90
Committee of the Whole, 65
common law, 21
Common Sense (Paine), 40–41
Concord (Massachusetts), 7–8, 36–37
Congregational Church, 23
Connecticut, 16, 23–24, 55, 69, 81
consent of the governed, 42
Constitution
amendment process, 84, 86, 88–89
amendments, 86, 88, 91
Bill of Rights, 7, 81, 84–85
judicial review, 89
preamble wording, 74, 76
presidents and boundaries of, 74
signing of, 76
Constitutional Convention
Benjamin Franklin and, 75
compromises, 70–73
convention rules, 68
debates, 70, 78
delegates, 62, 64
intellectual background of, 63
proposed, 61
ratification rules, 73–74
three-part national government, 66
Continental army
conditions, 43–44
payment of troops, 43
Washington chosen to lead, 38–39
Continental Congress, 35, 37–38, 40, 42–43, 49, 51, 63
Cornwallis, Charles, 48–49
corporate personhood, 90
Currency Act, 29

D
death penalty, 21–22
Debates in the Several State Conventions on the Adoption of the Federal Constitution (Elliot), 68
Declaration of Independence, 10, 42–45, 51, 54
Declaration of Rights and Grievances, 29
Delaware, 16–17, 19, 32, 45, 69, 81
democratic values
amendments to Constitution extended, 89–90
equality, 21, 42, 51–54, 88–89
local control over churches and, 23
de Pontgibaud, Chevalier, 47
Dutch colonists, 14, 16, 22

E
East India Company, 34
economy
after American Revolution, 51, 56, 58
after French and Indian War, 28
in colonial regions, 19
as issue in Constitutional Convention, 70, 72–73
Eddis, William, 18
education, 23–24, 89
Elliot, Jonathan, 68
England
compromise offered to, 38
French and Indian War and, 26–28
reaction to Boston Tea Party, 35
reluctance to declare independence from, 37
rights of individuals in, 20
taxes imposed by, 27–31, 33–34
taxes paid by citizens, 8, 28
See also American Revolution
Enlightenment, 24–25, 42, 65
equality
Constitution and, 88–89
in Declaration of Independence, 42
expanded meaning of, 51–54
religious discrimination and, 22–23
Equal Rights Amendment (ERA), 88
European discovery, 12–14

F
Federalist Papers, 77–78, 90
Federalists
characteristics of, 78–79
in state conventions, 81, 83
Fleming, Thomas, 29
Florida, 16, 27, 50
France
aid to revolutionaries, 46–47
colonies in North America, 13, 16
Franklin, Benjamin
Albany Plan and, 27
on Constitution, 75
Constitutional Convention and, 61–62, 69
Declaration of Independence and, 42
on making laws, 25
on signing Declaration of Independence, 43
signing of Constitution, 76
French and Indian War, 26–27

G
Gage, Thomas, 30, 36
Gaspee (British ship), 34
Gates, Horatio, 46
George III (king of England), 22, 26, 36, 39, 43, 45, 50
Georgia, 16, 32, 35, 48, 55,

64, 81
Gerry, Elbridge, 70, 76
government, in colonies
Britain reduced powers of, 35
duty to serve needs of individual, 42
Enlightenment and, 24–25, 65
Mayflower Compact, 15
religion and, 22–23
voting for representation, 29
government, in states
under Articles of Confederation, 51, 56
under Constitution, 70, 74
government, national
under Articles of Confederation, 55
under Constitution, 66–67
Granville, Earl, 25
Grayson, William, 83
Great Awakening, 22–23
Great Charter, 20
Green Mountain Boys, 37

H
Habeas Corpus Act, 20
Hamilton, Alexander
on Articles of Confederation, 60
at Constitutional Convention, 62, 69, 84
described, 64
Federalist Papers and, 77–78
Hamilton: An American Musical, 87
Hancock, John, 38, 43, 81, 82
Harvard University, 23
Haudenosaunee (Iroquois), 26
Henry, Patrick, 64, 83
Hessian troops, 45
Howe, William, 40, 46
Hughes, Charles Evans, 89

I
indentured servants, 16
independence
call for, by Paine, 40–42
declared, 42–43

J
Jamestown (Virginia), 6, 14
Jay, John, 64, 77
Jefferson, Thomas
Constitutional Convention and, 61, 64
Declaration of Independence and, 42
on government under Articles of Confederation, 57
Jews, 23
John (king of England), 20
Johnson, Paul, 23
judicial review, 89

K
King, Rufus, 69
King's College, 24
Knox, Henry, 37

L
land ownership, 20
Lee, Richard Henry, 42
Lexington (Massachusetts), 7–8, 36–37
Locke, John, 6, 24, 42

M
Madison, James
on Anti-Federalists, 78
Bill of Rights and, 84
Constitutional Convention and, 60–61, 65–66
Federalist Papers and, 77
Magna Carta, 20
Maryland, 16, 18, 23, 32, 39, 60, 61, 81, 83
Mason, George, 62, 76
Massachusetts
African Americans in, 54
farmers' rebellion in, 58
ratification convention, 81
Massachusetts Bay Colony, 6, 15–16
Mayflower Compact, 15
McCullough, David, 24, 44
Mee, Charles L., Jr., 62
middle colonies, 19
militias, 19, 36–38, 44, 58
Miranda, Lin-Manuel, 87
Montesquieu, 24
Montgomery, Richard, 40
Morison, Samuel Eliot, 31
Morris, Gouverneur, 67, 72, 76
Morris, Richard B., 22, 79

N
Native Americans
British territory reserved for, 28
Constitutional Convention and, 63
effect of colonization on, 12–14
lack of rights, 21
part of democratic community, 86
protection from, 19, 44, 58
natural rights, 24
navy established, 40
New Hampshire, 16, 23, 83
New Jersey, 16, 45, 55, 81
New Jersey Plan, 67, 69
New Netherland, 16
New York
battles in, 37, 45–46
English control, 16
French and Indian War and, 26
protests in, 35
religion in, 23
Stamp Act Congress and, 29
North, Lord
fall of government, 49
repeal of taxes and, 33
troops to crush rebellion sent by, 39, 40, 45
North Carolina
established, 16
ratification and, 84–85
religion in, 23
violence in, 48, 55

O

Oglethorpe, James, 16
Ohio River Valley, 26, 58
Old Deluder Laws, 23

P

Paine, Thomas, 40–42, 64
paper money
  under Articles of Confederation, 57
  British refusal to accept for taxes, 28–29
  for Continental army, 38
  lack of gold to back, 58
Paterson, William, 67, 69
Pennsylvania, 8, 16, 39, 45, 47, 55, 62, 67, 79, 81, 83
Pennsylvania Assembly, 25
Pennsylvania State House, 61, 65
Peters, William, 79, 84
Philadelphia (Pennsylvania),
  captured by Howe, 46
  conditions during summer 1787, 67
  description, 17, 19
  importance of, 18
  meetings in, 8, 35, 37, 43, 61–65, 77, 86, 90
  protests in, 35
  See also Constitutional Convention
Pinckney, Charles, 66
Pierce, William, 64
Pilgrims, 15
Pitt, William, 45
Plessy v. Ferguson, 89
Plymouth (Massachusetts), 14–15, 22
population
  pushed Native Americans out of homelands, 14
  of Native Americans wiped out, 13
  Virginia Plan and, 67, 69
  voting under Articles of Confederation and, 56
Preston, Thomas, 33
Princeton University, 24, 45
Puritans, 6, 15–16, 23, 32

Q

Quakers, 16, 31
Quartering Acts, 28, 31, 35

R

Ramsay, David, 53
Randolph, Edmund
  as Federalist, 83
  Jefferson's letter to, 57
  on language in Constitution, 90
  refusal to sign Constitution, 76
  Virginia Plan proposed by, 65–66
ratification
  Articles of Confederation and, 51
  of amendments, 85, 88–89
  order of states for Constitution, 79, 81, 83–84
  process of, 73–74
  public debate over, 78–79
  song, 82
  support for, 77
religion
  Bill of Rights and, 11, 85
  development of American identity and, 21–22
  discrimination based on, 22
  education and, 23–24
  Enlightenment and, 24
  First Amendment, 85
Revere, Paul, 36
Rhode Island
  Constitutional Convention and, 62
  Gaspee and, 34
  ratification and, 84–85
Royal Navy, 28
Royal Proclamation of 1763, 28
Rush, Benjamin, 44
Rutledge, John, 72

S

Santa Clara County v. Southern Pacific Railroad Co., 90
Saratoga (New York), 46–48
Scott, Dred, 90
segregation, 89
separation of powers, 24
Shays, Daniel, 58
Shays's Rebellion, 58–59
Sherman, Roger, 69–70
slavery
  after American Revolution, 53–54
  in colonies, 16, 19
  counted in Constitution, 70
  debated at Constitutional Convention, 72–73, 79, 83
  lack of rights, 21
  outlawed by 13th Amendment, 9, 88
  Supreme Court decisions about, 90
Smith, John, 14
Sons of Liberty, 30
South Carolina, 16, 23, 32, 40, 48, 53, 55, 66, 70, 72, 83
southern colonies, 19
Spain
  colonies, 13–14
  fear of alliance with, 57
  France's reward to, 27
  war on Britain, 47
speech, evolution of, 18
Stamp Act, 29–31
Stamp Act Congress, 29, 31
Sugar Act, 28–29
Supreme Court, 10–11, 64, 86, 89–90
Swedish colonists, 13, 16

T

taxes, colonial era
  imposed by England, 27–31, 33–34
  paid by citizens, 8, 28
taxes under Articles of Confederation, 56
taxes under Constitution, 70, 72

tea, 31, 34–35
tobacco, 14, 19
Townshend, Charles, 31
Townshend Acts, 31–33
trade
under Articles of Confederation, 55
boycotts, 31–32, 35
with England, 19, 33, 40, 58
Travels Through the Middle Settlements in North America in the Years 1759 and 1760 (Burnaby), 17
Trenton (New Jersey), 44–45
trial rights, 20, 85
Tucker, Josiah, 55
Two-House Plan, 69–70

V

Valley Forge (Pennsylvania), 47
Virginia, 14–16, 21–23, 38–39, 42, 48, 55, 60–62, 64–65, 74, 83–84
Virginia Declaration of Rights, 62
Virginia Plan, 66–67, 69, 73, 76
voting
bans from, 23
for colonial governments, 29
English rights and land ownership, 20
rights after American Revolution, 53
rights extended by amendments to Constitution, 9, 88

W

Washington, George
attack on Trenton, 44–45
battles with Howe, 46
Battle of Yorktown, 48–49
chosen president, 84
Constitutional Convention and, 62–63, 65, 78
Continental army and, 37–39, 43, 45
First Continental Congress and, 35
on government under Articles of Confederation, 58
weapons
in Bill of Rights, 10, 85
at Concord and Lexington, 36
for American Revolution, 37, 48
westward migration, 28
Whitefield, George, 22–23
Winthrop, John, 16
writs of assistance, 28
Wythe, George, 65

Y

Yale University, 23

Z

Zinn, Howard, 30

Picture Credits

Cover, pp. 60, 84 GraphicaArtis/Contributor/Archive Photos/Getty Images; pp. 4–5, 6 (top), 13, 15, 20, 59, 89 Bettmann/Contributor/Bettmann/Getty Images; pp. 6 (bottom left), 7 (top left), 7 (bottom left), 9, 30, 46, 54, 69, 78, 88 Courtesy of the Library of Congress; p. 6 (bottom right) Georgios Kollidas/Shutterstock.com; p. 7 (top right) Smith Collection/Gado/Contributor/Archive Photos/Getty Images; pp. 7 (bottom left), 43, 52, 56, 66, 81, 85 Courtesy of the National Archives; p. 7 (bottom right) Hulton Archive/Stringer/Hulton Archive/Getty Images; p. 10 Joe Ravi/Shutterstock.com; pp. 17, 25 Stock Montage/Contributor/Archive Photos/Getty Images; p. 19 Courtesy of Encyclopedia Britannica; pp. 22, 75 Everett Historical/Shutterstock.com; p. 27 MPI/Stringer/Archive Photos/Getty Images; p. 31 Hulton Archive/Stringer/Archive Photos/Getty Images; p. 32 Courtesy of The New York Public Library Digital Collections; p. 34 Edward Gooch/Stringer/Hulton Archive/Getty Images; pp. 38, 63 DEA PICTURE LIBRARY/Contributor/De Agostini/Getty Images; p. 40 Hulton Archive/Staff/Hulton Archive/Getty Images; p. 48 DEA/M. SEEMULLER/Getty Images; p. 49 joe arrigo/Shutterstock.com; p. 61 f11photo/Shutterstock.com; p. 65 Universal History Archive/Contributor/Universal Images Group/Getty Images; p. 71 Orhan Cam/Shutterstock.com; p. 72 MANDEL NGAN/Staff/AFP/Getty Images; p. 87 Theo Wargo/Staff/Getty Images Entertainment/Getty Images; p. 91 Pacific Press/Contributor/LightRocket/Getty Images.

About the Author

Leslie Beckett has written several books for children and young adults on topics that include American history, government, and citizenship. She graduated from college with dual degrees in political science and women's studies, and she has always had a passion for volunteering and activism. When she is not writing, she enjoys traveling to national parks with her husband and three children, and she loves reading, especially political biographies and mysteries.